mezzaluna

Also by Michele Leggott

Poetry
Vanishing Points (2017)
Heartland (2014)
Mirabile Dictu (2009)
Journey to Portugal (2007)
Milk & Honey (New Zealand 2005, United Kingdom 2006)
As far as I can see (1999)
DIA (1994)
Swimmers, Dancers (1991)
Like This? (1988)

Criticism
Reading Zukofsky's 80 Flowers (1989)

As Editor
with coeditor Martin Edmond, *Beyond the Ohlala Mountains: Poems 1968–2002*
    by Alan Brunton (2013)
Young Knowledge: The Poems of Robin Hyde (2003)
with Alan Brunton and Murray Edmond, *Big Smoke: New Zealand Poems*
    1960–1975 (2000)
The Book of Nadath by Robin Hyde (1999)
The Victory Hymn by Robin Hyde (1995)

Audio Recording
Michele Leggott: New Zealand Poets, The Laureate Series (2009)

Wesleyan University Press   Middletown, Connecticut

selected poems

MEZZALUNA

Michele Leggott

Wesleyan University Press
Middletown CT 06459
www.wesleyan.edu/wespress

Manufactured in the United States of America
Designed by Mindy Basinger Hill
Illustration by Gabrielle Olivia Hill
Typeset in Adobe Caslon Pro

Library of Congress Cataloging-in-Publication Data

Names: Leggott, Michele J., author.

Title: Mezzaluna : selected poems / Michele Leggott.

Description: Middletown, CT : Wesleyan University Press, [2020] |
Series: Wesleyan poetry | Summary: "The selected poems
of award-winning and critically acclaimed New Zealand poet
Michele Leggott" — Provided by publisher.

Identifiers: LCCN 2019033201 (print) | LCCN 2019033202 (ebook) |
ISBN 9780819579072 (paperback) | ISBN 9780819579089 (ebook)

Classification: LCC PR9639.3.L45 A6 2020 (print) |
LCC PR9639.3.L45 (ebook) | DDC 821/.914—dc23

LC record available at https://lccn.loc.gov/2019033201

LC ebook record available at https://lccn.loc.gov/2019033202

5   4   3   2   1

for those who travel light and lift darkness

Contents

like this?

on white you fall
into line
            her voice fills
the ground
potato cuts
            the sun
dries paints
            the deck prints
shapes shadows
of oranges
            green
            'cyan and
            magenta'
                  sail
      your picnic
sea
    into the eye
    land crimson
    lemons
            hand me
the moon
risen rode
            rose ride
white
      out to see

Watermelon World

she sings fish are jumping
in your room birds ride

around the walls pink is
picking up white cotton

is high diamonds rose and
why one of these days

the picture may be painted
melons sent flying hearts

and stars harm nothing you
care about more than today

signature pink, leap
bodily the helix enough
doubled erotic or singing to
say I am energy make
certain my best feints dab
your ever, this is me

An Island

An island for Easter   an Easter island
in the pacific Pacific
                of the Inside Passage

                grounding the dream and dreaming the ground
                with the Sunshine Crew
                                        that's daffodils
    and a shack on the water   whatever the dream hands out
    whatever we can bring
    what
        ever
            these spring nights no-one can sleep   days set to roll over
            showing long flanks and a bright mammalian eye

Other imaginations fired easily and here we are
headed straight into history
                other stories breathing   spaces
                                        between the quotidian hauls and the junk we saved
        a walk out to the plane at infinity
        or a face turned south smiling meridian coordinates
                                        at the sun   *oh merry days*
great circles roll over our heads and we're breathing even so
the fish can't tell if it's
                air like water
    or *water like air*
            nosing in among the sailing islands
            whose hills roll in the gentle swell of the Gulf of

Georgia   you sent us a west wind and Florence saying
welcome to Roseland   here comes the water
                                back up the bay through the fruit trees
                coming into leaf

walnuts   apples   veranda   pear around the corner
                              mad with blossom and
the high diver who danced courtship on dynamo wings
                                        all weekend
                    long
                              in the orchard
          which blew its own scents and those
          of the rock breaker
                         elusive   unlikely   unreal
                                                  to us
               in the green   cinnamon   evening

Canoe   sun   showers   arbutus   dropping those honey flowers
into the sea
               bird of the other laugh circling above them
                                        and out on the point
                              cabins breathe in the trees
          with the help of that redesigning wind
the pictures we wanted to paint badly
will be tacked up
               robin's egg tender with the yellow blown out
               hearts and stars and squalls
                              rattling through a silver-pen narrative
               the strait can do to a count of minutes   (fast passages
or ricepaper wash
white sheets and open doors
                    on closed eyelids (the dream)   (the curve
                                        of a dyed egg
                              a hemisphere
               or a line of longitude
               my ache for yours
                         trading in the dim cabins of possibility
                         for the wingspread facts

                                                of the dream
                                    and so
            the whales came in like the naturals they were
            throwing off rowboats of improbability
                                they travelled west with the sailing islands
                    the world turned some more
and both archipelagos
came up for air
            gulf and pool
                    and eye of the wind *palagi* blue
                                        grey
                                    green
                                gulps
                                of Pacific lilac and the wild red currant
                                around the headlands
                                            flowers on the water
                                or
                                    signs of the pace we set

The dark pointer has an Easter face and northwest light
is flooding that outflung arm
                            of the sea   sun gone over the edge
                            or beyond the hills of the bay
she called him the Sentinel
and he stands between us and the wet   light   of   the   Pacific
                            islands like the moon passing through a phase
            he guards this passage
    perhaps us

    nights in the cabin with the kids asleep underfoot
    or listening in the dark
                        days running for the tops of hills
                                        the ends of points
                        any place a line might sail in

(that curve

          breathing tenderness saying   we are so close
          need so much

             so many times over

we keep moving tangling the lines
and the great distances grow dangerous

          unless the wind on your face
          is also my breath

             in the hollow of your throat
          and we go on like that

       forever

     for good

       times   feet on the porch rail in the late sun
       roasting paschal lamb stuck with rosemary

           waiting for the others

       the canoe the car

           the crab-catchers line-casters lake-finders

the shore-walkers bird-watchers book-readers

           letter-writers lily-sniffers

 snake-chasers shell-hunters egg-painters

the eaters of spice buns and bacon

        (the Sunshine Breakfast warm at the oven door
        phenomenal scrambled eggs

     the whole crew

       coming in now

           dice-rollers gin-drinkers hangovers

     crowded round the table again
     light on their faces reflected Pacific

          morning's say-so

    or the sweet chiaroscuro of candles

           orange skins thrown on the fire

     wood brought in for the night

under the skewed eyes of the woodgrain beast
whose portrait hangs over the hearth

       bear   dog   coyote

or ocean chart for those who flunked the tacky gestalt
who saw only stars
who took islands as they came

here

here

here

and here

and had to be shown   eyes   nose   mouth   (Pacific spaces

or head
fins
tail
Te ika a Māui
or the navel of the world away off to the south there
Te pito o te henua
attached by the cords of memory and desire
to the improbable the very delicate the invincible
beginning
'my' Easter island

Show me the star charts and I will show you
plans for a future hung between Georgia and Hauraki
Auckland and Valparaiso
Easter and Pender
place where the whales came in
and
space where they used to sing
a future the shape of a bellied sail

twenty eight names for the winds of Rapa Nui

and what matters is the distance they're blowing into the sail
that it be navigable
                    to the mind wanting voices   (the mid-ocean gam
                    gathering word
                              from wherever   whatever
                                        walking out on mnemonic extremities
                                        eyes   nose   mouth   navel
              to the plane at infinity
              takeoff!

                         The bird-men of Easter Island were egg thieves
                         and so are we
                                        out in the orchard where the kids hunt what's left
                                        of the chocolate cache
                                                  among the dripping trees

                                   in cold spring
         I lie awake before sunrise
               even breathing and eyelid curves all around
                         the crew is dreaming of crabmeat salads and exorbitant lamb
         and somehow

a fantasm of island raspberries and double cream gets into the picture
with a flourish of past summerings
                              and the whiff of a biddable future   (is it greed
              or appetite
                         has us out wading the terraces again for the big red crabs
                                   basking on beds of gently waving sea-lettuce
       which turns a wistful eye on the great shells
       left by the ebb on the bottom of Ella Bay?
                              a bed of grandaddy clams out there

feasts and delicacies
we come back for
                    singling out
                                making sense (and love
                    of the things
                    we find
                                getting hungrier by the moment
                    or maybe just sure of the victualling stops

        I'm happy I'm afraid

Emily's Sentinel looks out on the sea
and that (improbable) arm has kept the blackbirders out
                                        the depopulators of small paradises
            the grid-men with their hands-on madness
            who have also covered the Pacific spaces (hold it right there
                                    and might one day come in close (don't
                                                    move a mussel
                        to make us an offer we can't refuse
            then say

goodbye to the beloved junk the holidays out of cardboard boxes
off weekend crockery
            in good company
                        goodbye to the voyages the small paradises the bellying sail
                        goodbye   and would you let it happen

                    just catch an early boat and never   look   back?

Within the month we passed close to the island again
put a glass on the bay and saw
                    a flag snapping on the whitewood pole of the point
                                                        hola!

and the panorama moved right along so that next it was
Roseland's cabins vanishing
                                    into the leafed-over orchard
                so green   so sunlit
                minimal kinetic glitter in the dancing glass

and the same wind rolling the clouds back off heaven that night
would have shown us the first of ten moons
                                    sliding up over the islands   phasing in
                the time of our lives
                could have told us that love's growing season
                                                    was making another start

                a second heart begins to beat
                                                    close to the first

Withywind

there will be a story

darkening in the throat
deeper at the edges (now)

wind winds a wound
things we used to do

in this place
                    not this time
though
            winds wind

the traveller returning, welcome
and breath

of hemispheric summers

drudgery the clematis
overlooks
                    and star wistaria
                    staring

when you were young,
honeysuckle
                    there was always
                    milk
                                and that
witloose trelliswork
I was busy with

wind

words come so slowly
it has been lonely
                    a phoenix palm
                    and behind it
                                   crystalline glitter
another story, waving

plantain *paradisiaca* a bird
musey with waves
Helicon a harbour cone
here
      bright
              Greek
                    over Narrowneck:

head each I am
                   sweet snow
                   now
kahili ginger
on a jungle coast
the space junk sails at will

oh hello

think this
into abalone

nacre no body
embraces

acheless or
necklace

wrack free
breaks

reckless
that kissed

detritus whist
forsake and

dance
unsounded

fortune on
wild waves

forsake and
leviathan

never
look back

at the smash
nacreous

deeps
unless

eyes crescent
swimming

ascent

Road Music

Just when you think you've made it
out of the bosom

you go back alone
your child asleep in the back

and the road is jammed with ghost Peugeots
grinding over the Mahoenuis
cornering with you in the gorge
                                          the stories burgeon
flying along the coast   the parallel track
a two-tone blast at the top of Mount Messenger

brief dark of the tunnel
where the clock turns over

Coming and going the ghosts travel with you
they overlay your rest

it's her voice calls your child in the pissy Ladies'
at Te Kūiti (Teka Witi)
his red sweater your jersey
your kiss her Kodachrome lipstick
(she hated the song)

the milkshakes are daylight robbery   the car plants groves
of plumstone trees   the seats go down
at night and the shorter child sleeps on the driver's side
the cabbages fell of the truck they said
at this corner   the very elegant coast of the northern bight
is Monterey   your father is the best driver
in the world
                coming or going
                how we would have driven that coast
your watercolour eyes make it into the scrub in time

a bird wekas off the road with inches to spare
a miss is as good as a mile

This time the white Peugeot
gets there with the rain and tails Datsuns
freighting kids home from winter term
or music lessons
                    the barley broth is in its third day
boiled clean of its bones   thick
with orthodoxy the spoons dredge up and convey
to mouths that have learned a rich language
of gristle and fat

you go out for tea and miss
this last detail of what is utterly familiar

will your boy thank you
for any of this?
                    did you thank them?

or Beryl and Pat and Joyce
who feed you both and put up with his eighteen months?

You come back loaded with grapefruit, jam, corned beef
a case of green wine
                    and all the letters you wrote from years ago

it's an evening warm as your unfinished conversation
lovely to come back to
all the shops are open but he only wants to watch the rocket ride
phoenix crowns whirl overhead
the fish shop has smoked kingfish wings and a hāpuku head
sweet smoky meat
eye delicacies and fin struts to fly on home
and get started again

small and affordable change of season
brings pineapples from the Cooks into the shops
just ahead of Gala apples
there's a tree in the back yard might be Gala
loaded
he eats off it every day as the wind freshens
pineapple sliced behind the picture window
a boat called Rhyme is beating up the harbour
one on the tree one in the fridge
he's got it straight already

luxuriance when the power goes off
bodies slip around after the soap the turtle boats and teacups
gleaming by candle-lantern
a song about honey and money another about a hum (a hum)
the mockingbird lullaby that never worked
not everything clears but his names tumble past in the dark
remembering womb and water embrace

there's holding on (hello) and letting go (goodbye)
there's getting to the beach and back
Commando M's with the stink cut out and toes poking through
eloquence
then there's that conversation pulling on an old sweater now
still waiting as he bangs knife against plate against bowl against cup
an exaltation of toast
big honey on he shrieks I want helping

last night the Silver Slocan nearly beat down the door
its skinny holiday glitter
that air of early Macs Doukhobor cooking and aspens on fire
anticipation of course
Valhalla bacon Lemon Creek Lodge and the cheapie off the window
in New Denver
the map in the head with its unsuspected throughroads
lakes he was changed on the hood of the car in front of
just like, we say and didn't the time fly

the last stanza almost doesn't make it
leaps the rising gangplank longlegged pigheaded pleased
to be on board
enjoys the trip the weather the drift into the other end
the new menu will keep
five minutes creased already it rides in a back pocket
reading itself for signs of
his sleeping cheek

Garbo in a Gown

it's been a pretty ordinary day
I never saw you look like that before
what bit of brilliance gets its start standing in a fruit bowl?
the play should peel tragedy like an orange
she said, and squirt you in the eye
look at me like that
or explode tamarillos under your feet—a little bit of rubbish
it's not a theory it's a story
I got up this morning in the dark and heard the cameras
your eyes your eyes—
laughlines, remember?

ran the movie mid-afternoon it left me aching
looked at the moon high up where ice was cracking unseeable stars
ran after you through snow for the kiss
the one of course that blows it all apart—
was that the deeply satisfying meaning of the white dress?
laugh and cry and don't sleep she said
it went away—it never went away—it was never real—here it is now
sailing the strait straight out of a sunshine breakfast
persevering, wind whipping my face—my hair your face
was it really that long or did you stand closer
than memory allows? what about the trip back to town?
sweet little things in my ears

it's the sports car through Paris
or mandarin weather right on your sunny doorstep
the half-worlds meet and make it up as they go
first persons second persons third persons
a few irresponsible demonstratives, movie flex perfect
flip tail mad, the gown that hangs in here
(tapping her head, right side) its versions
of the same conversations we're still stepping into

tingling fingers five minutes into the wintertime dishes
(real warmth) where's my staircase? is the engine running?
the light in your eyes the way your smile just beams
upside the way you sing off-key
down among the unmade beds the washing the cleaning up
orange peel exploded tamarillo (the carpet the duvet)
pulp, pips, play—still hear the cameras?

Harry Ariadne, your footsteps pace mine
you walk down the hall with me and laugh at absurdities
this hush that the poet is writing again
winged circuits flown by those anecdotal doves
somebody lets out down near the waterfront each morning
you can imagine the sight the whirring
bicameral possibilities exploding everywhere
she knows without looking in the mirror she's wearing
the dangerous face knows without looking at the tears in the gown
that its roses and unicorns will go on precluding sleep
and smooth getaways   she walks out the door
in her pocket there's a small bright orange

swimmers, dancers

Dear Heart

dear heart it was a coast road
long past lilac time and well out of town
                                the sea out of sight   and driving north
                              in the far south the radio swelled
                  nostalgia
                  and I want you to know
                                  that I remember it all   the time
it was 'just' part of your afternoon repertoire
a dance-floor pick-up
                    kept on at you all those years   the romance the real
                  life dance we were brought in to share
       the sun and the son
       you were making it true with a late-fifties step
                                  up the coast   into heaven
                and some memorable parties
                fishing trips
                      carnivals
                                a dog   a truck   a baby sister
             a walk to the swing bridge
     and back
            and more . . .

                then it was moving into town   settling
                down and later the piano
                                        you were picking out Mancini arrangements
Nat King Cole My Fair Lady and the theme
from Mondo Cane
                you sang them into the woodwork
                and when it really was
                                        a table for one and a single rose
                                        that hard lost time
        I heard Errol Garner play I only
        have eyes for you in a winter house   dancing
                                                with knots in my throat past midnight
                and your brave tra-la-la
        half a world away
                        it's a lonely thing to do
                        and you couldn't get used to the cold
                                                        or the hole in the bed
                        the silence after you sang out
                        the songs that would never mean dancing again
        oh my sentimental mother

you died

and I saw you in each other's arms again

                              an hour from dawn

        just as it should have been

    my dear

        I took your rings and came back to the real

        life dance of these years

                        a song by songs and it seems I don't know all the words

                        because you never did

                                        but

    here we are driving the coasts of our dreams and

    bending again in time

                        over the precious cradle of the heart

Colloquy

virgins plus curtains minus dots claret and celestial blue

people still go to cottages in moody seaside weather
to read for a week   how will we do it now?

when I go for walks words stalk along too
I'll be travelling mid-February and can't guarantee a lucid mind

what about a big table in a room with windows
looking over the wild and wavy event?

or good merganser fans unfolding folding thought out there

one of these days we'll tend to them
those fair fictitious people the women

Oldest and Most Loyal American Friend

more to our liking—
the idea of a winged victory
headless to be sure

but lucidly and in good humor
she'll answer our questions:
when did the line begin

to curve underwater like that?
why are the roses (which aren't
even here) suddenly twisting

into circles? why are we drawn
to these figures? Samothrace
you've vanished

in your place, le juste milieu,
Gertrude stalks
the little lobsters of Perpignan

replaces the bright water with
a clear chablis she'll drink
them with tonight

make a feast of tumult eat
its flesh crack the golden shell
and suck confusion's juice

wet ankles tucked-up skirt
prismatic drops in the bucket
on the stolen stele

knock   it   off

fish   it   out

2

Common cheap and tender
the pleasure of a purely predatory
recipe, say crawfish étouffée

we were seduced at once by
the little town (no poetry) and thought
what a happy life it would be

only to cultivate white
raspberries (sea also) iced
champagne by the approved method

then go to the Lyric Restaurant
drink solstitial dazzle on the terrace
and order the house specialty

you'll wait an hour but it will fly
hot dry white wine, bouquet and bouillon
the rifts and the tears are your own

in the interstices of the lobster meat
a rich dark roux from which the bouquet
may be removed   They did not in Perpignan

Reading Zukofsky's 80 Flowers

lavenders blue
roll your eleven weeks onto summer's late belly and look out
at the world with your black olive eyes
this was promised under the apple tree at Christmas
when you swam in deep pools of picture space nine days out
among the dream polaroids jacaranda diamante
simulacra of before and after
the visceral rub of pōhutukawa in bloom
good established labour the sun going down the Carmel geese
shrieking and flocking the big movie of us coming apart then
waterboatmen on the lake at dawn
and we began the long haul from Recovery nine floors up
to Tranquility a sea *a somer-séson*

all the pretty little horses pretty things pretty soon
the goodnight fine art getting
the lullaby to work the baby to sleep *merrigolds* he smiles tell me
another one and the story remembers itself by rhyme settles easily
into songs he likes the made-up rock
and roll the stroller doing its stationary miles in the next room
the two of them the two of us too whacked to
(what??) read proof
quote dear one sweet heart lover unquote air of heaven
half hyphen moon bee time energy colon coffee colon
the feeds the changes the drinks of water the *spiders* on the cistern
nightlife Horace and Chick Corea at it again
in the lamplight heliotrope splash! mother of thyme stomma cock

mares nest and moonshine wakerobin oh yes
and again and again the all-night frogs go la-di-da-di-dah
to the tune of John Brown's body
the household gets up at midnight and stirs about
paradise garden I would write you down he said
in a style of leaves growing
eyes curving
toward that question just where do the roses swing
are they pink and blown and warm as sleep
at the gate where lavender works the bees all year round
or red and sweet as tea grown cool because everyone went to check
some story about *wind roses* you already knew were lining the nest
with scent and bloom and two quarter-view profiles
flickering out of the frame

Boosey & Hawkes
Black & Decker where do we get to
slow nights when the book clears off to Baltimore *unimaginable*
in the time of tearwater tea and willpower cookies
Hobans Ahlbergs Lobel Wise Brown I Can Read
two wind-ups with outstretched arms and joined hands
dancing around and around the parameters
goor jaggery plums and palm sugar
dates with stratagems the minute hand sweeps away
some things have to be written in later some things
look like porcelain fingers on the coverlet *unforgettable*
inhabitation the moment hand-painted plaster of pearls
some things to be said for low orbit

cosmos nods
Hippolyte and Cornelia rumble over the picket
which line is his? which hers? moonbeam you smile around
then again *it is not night when I see your face* thefts modifying
or migrating winging along close to a shelving coast
where the expedition has wandered out of its hinterlands at last
whooping like kids walking on sand dollars at dead low tide
a stone's throw from the lacewing villas way on out to the channel
sea biscuits cake urchins (placenta to you) walking on the sea bed
the rider in the backpack wants to bite them all
mouthfuls of breast and he doesn't care if it's salty
he cries out and when he gets what he wants we'll be there
Mare Tranquilitum see horse the flowers

Merylyn or Tile Slide or Melete

I've fed the baby and put him down   it's eleven ten
winds like trades sweep the phoenixes   high airs for highchairs
a story of palimpsest and simulacra a house of replicas
writing over its fictions sticking them on the machine hitting PRINT
and away it goes
over the rooftops the thrashing pompadours the stunt kites that whistle and hum
their lines   in contemplation of the image
templum a shape to bite   with   they are very close
pleasure   they share genetic material they could be coeval
                          they speak together they've travelled from the same place
                          so when one slides back to the power station she is pleased
finessed a   by the return THAT'S MY SLIDE she says
projector   a good one I'll loan you details help yourself
                     the real thing THE SIGNIFICANT OTHER is up at the gallery
                     Julian's hung the tiles sideways STET but Alexa has my letter
                                                                  as if I
put the baby slides through as well TENDERNESS
reading one face in the other
dear Flossie Teacake   Posy Fossil   Sugarplum   phantoms
a fall   ARE ALWAYS INTERESTING they warm by association
of raw sugar in the demerara jar   is always a space
December filling up again he's turning one   marked out
sweet darling one standing by the peg basket by himself   a
waves of applause steady   piece of ground set apart a shape
as she goes   cut out for travel through a number of worlds

happens   what I can do where I can go what they can give
here   and what they keep me from
                    ESTABLISHES FOCAL LENGTH sitting in the dark five years old
                    optician's glasses testing testing cold hit precision and footnotes
                    m a g n i f i c a t i o n sharp edges bright lights in the dark
                    I can feed him change him put him down feel my way back
can it be done?   to sleep thinking
who by?   SUBVERT OR OBSCURE EXISTENCE OF THE NARRATIVE
who?   POSITION
she gave me *cut lunch* a blank cheque also volumes of information
he heard me get out the cutting board and say   LET'S EAT
                    THE WOMAN OUTSIDE THE ART GALLERY SELLING AVOCADOS
                    muscle   carapace   flesh   position   action —
push your fingers in
the secret folds of semi-soft sculpture BLUSHING SHAPE
CREAMED TONGUE PUFFS THE ROSE AND STAR a world of wonder high fidelity
sweeping with the phoenix feather palms thrashing
taking eating having layering icing on the CAKE
when he gets back   lemon angel surprises
oh   the hell out of tartan touring with Betty
petit   from the deck of the Earnslaw binoculars in hand REMARKABLE
berceau   what is to be seen once the soft interiorities
marlin boats at Whitianga   of the voice strike out instruction
identifying the Douglas Fir at Lac Maligne   bye sunshines
CHANGED HER TACK went horseback riding left them squinting at a sail

sobriety sobriquet, girls   lost heart
SHE OPENED HER FIRST ONE-MAN EXHIBITION   today
AT THE LABYRINTH GALLERY   the old question (the cake stalls) (ack)
can history do more than amuse? replies A MUSE does it better
rewrites replays returns TIMES OF OUR SOCIALISATION   see it now
                    underfoot together on the kitchen floor crawling over diamonds
                    and squares (Mondrian a cinch later on) crosseyed with the effort of
                         ESTABLISHING FOCAL LENGTH and tearing up yes newsprint
NO   laid down against the flood the bin the cooker the cat's plate
clouds   the epic defrost the highchair detritus three times a day
                         or just grubby rage for activity a bit of fun SOME
flooral tile on the wall wall   ELEMENTARY GAME accountability
paper on the tiles SLIPPERY humming with xerox
and saving the text and blowing it up and staging repeats
MERYLYN SLIDES critical vocals ACCREDITED AS A POET   was a
does that   person in a pointy hat
square   simpering it's the way you hold your mouth
like BARE   around the word PO-
FACED lies there on the page HEY ROSEBUD little
bottom your mom's goodlooking a sundried nappy straight off the
line folds one through four two pins and away   sweep
she'd sooner be doing this   of the printer left to right right
critical fiction   to left pull on the line when interpolation breaks
in   into the digit count cursor hauling you over a landscape
florescence   whose every window fluoresces at a touch

where's Nicola? where's Betty? under the resin   tear
folding napkins with Mrs B studying the butter finger the power   away
a transitive verb has to EAT everything in its way   s
she bosses it (vanishes) BUT IF NOTHING HAS BEEN TAKEN
A WAY VERY MUCH HAS BEEN ADDED the baby in his berceaunette
SHOWING CLEARLY HOW EVERY FOLD IS MADE in terms of pink creases
a body of knowledge   Bella   Merylyn   meet Janet
                    she's wrapping the folks remarks in flimsy tissue WE SET THE STALL UP
                        ON THE LIBRARY STEPS BESIDE A TRESTLE GROANING WITH
                                DONATED FAIRY CAKE dispensed vital signs
        NO   NO   NO   NO   NO   NO
steaming   wringing   scrubbing   operas   AMALGAMATION
                                                    the glue that holds it together
many   soft interiorities musculature a growing body carefully
happy   as the boy Ambrosius and will
hours   when he's covered his new school books with yes wallpaper
                        a fight about pattern competence (pigheadedness) WELL YOU DO IT
pinning   THEN she stays up late ruling cutting pasting
pattern   at the end there's a little pile of damp books to be pressed
pieces   under THE BOOKS OF KNOWLEDGE volumes one through six
                                                            dry and wrinkle-free
she's filling handbags   in the morning
with plaster of Paris   IT TOOK THREE OR FOUR MINUTES BUT I MADE IT
to go on the wall   IT TOOK A LONG TIME but the family is full
next   of December babies tenor and vehicle they all resist

Tigers

                         wavejumping
              down the coast   a
           eight months a year call up   step
          the weather office every morning   into
         second-guess the winds at the cape   heaven
              at Kina Rd   deliberate
      the swell   more coffee a look around the windows
   west sou'west getting up now   more avocado on toast
            good thing that long season on Hass
   why settle for less   the best avo the best coast
   another balanced judgement   the best driver in the world
   from those who should know (best)   load up Bluey and go
          nose into the slipstream that may or may not be worth it
   he learned in the summer of cold southerlies we all   remember
   he was out   fierce concentration   it was strange
   in the waves   pulling in the new as the old   weather
   when she died   stripped heart and sail from him   then
        late on a windy afternoon in January   she just stopped
      one of those days around the bed   breathing
        he said to us   back there in the house on the hill
          I'm going   after scares vigils the descent
            to blow glass   hyaline   and its stations
          oh   WAVE, DURABLE FIRE   she'd gone
                yes   A SEA AZURE A CLEAR SKY
              and went off to measure up
                   the workshop

                    a pot of tea
        at six o'clock   vantage
      a quiet smoke looking at   points
       the day beginning   dear Phoeb it's
      black as the proverbial   or almost sunrise
       you could reach out and touch the mountain
     bare maybe   funny and unpredictable
    or snow down to the ranges   any time of year   some
    I'll be very low key he said   horsetrading
      at least   JACKIE V. THE BANDITS   a bloody performance
    for starters   workboots on the stairs   Jack at his shirtiest
    read   guns smoking in the manager's office   best
    about it   the rushes show them all shaking hands afterwards
    at Lucy's Gully the redwoods wave about   but he's gone
    in powerful upper airs   she was the only one saw him go
    in the grove itself   break apart in her arms
    shelter   she didn't MISS a thing   the tears
    he might have courted her there   POLYVALENCE   came
      a Taranaki girl from way back   into her heart
      good at connections   a survivor   then she called us
       you aren't going to hear   these shapes (snarl)
        but here you are   reading them
         right onto it   touch and turn   around
       half a world away he's there   don't
         take it too hard   cry now
                  Phoebe dear

41

                    dear bird
          there it is   stormy locus
          MATER CARA   of your conception
       she who is beloved   chick you are care
       staying up late   and it will keep you
       again   the sailors   take care   nestling
     Mother Carey   call you   your stars prove gentle
     a lineal sign   out in the waves   singing NOW
     to kick away   WELCOM SOMER WITH THY SONNE SOFTE
   suckling   from   this time he's gone to learn   (huh)
   they knead the soft belly   from Master Lino   one's
   fierce   they tear   (the best)   good two
   tiger eyes   then spring off   swinging   better get them
   lock   away   planetary   December babies all
   that perfect distance from   rings   three a   pride
   down curve when   her   off the punty   of tigers
     The Child sets in   turn around and   full eyes
     drives deeps and skies   planetary   it's done   like
     winds howling around the tank   reading painting
       Mercator's world isn't everything there is   pictures
       aerodynamically the   old lingua letters
         edge   a set of reef breaks   singing
       where   four metre faces   HO the tiger
         someone is   ~~at~~tempting   the
             always   nemesis
                cutting loose

dia

"Where exactly are we?"

INCANDESCENT LACUNAE FLUORESCE AT A
TOUCH **DESIRE** TORQUES DILOQUENT PEARL
CURVES LUMENS CON BRIO ALIGHT NO BODY
EMBRACES ACHELESS **DESIRE** ELSE NOT
SENSE MY GARDENS LAMELLAE TO BEE
DESIDERATE MOUTH BRIGHT ALMOND
ABEILLE AMYGDALA AH OH ORIOLES
ROSEATE SANGLOTS LIKE LITT**ORAL** COMEDY
SWEET AND PELAGIC AMEN ONTO LOGICAL
DELIQUESCENCE OR LICKETY SPIT **DELIGHT**
FISHTAILS DEEP TROPES SQUIRT SQUID SUCK
OCTOPI PULL ANEMONES GULP AURELIA
GASPS GOOSEBERRY VISCERA HOOT
COELENTERATE SOUP SIP SUP FOLLOW HER UP
SPIRULA SPIRULA THE HARD BIT IS GETTING
ASHORE WITH YOUR HYDROPHILE PURLING
DELIGHT INCUNABULA RAPT IN THE DARK
WITH**OUT**

Micromelismata

```
           micro      a    say
       coo melis  kiss  &   to      see   a
       coo  & effortless to me    bee white
       coo ee so be it in   oh yes  big noise
       print m & is in my   no I print   you       we
         an em in your ear & my kiss   can  I  say
       an iris & on I read raw  sh h sh know  leave  &
         em  on e  o & look shark  so  &   o h   then daunce
     seeing her  moment hear  melodiously on   it          for
       to her you are  such nice ass   for  isis desiring a
    to     & & do   a  little   oh  s   o    gloss strawberry
    be  melisma like    noises oh             loquat   orbiting
    so   no  sunlight     oh &               os etc        mist
   soft I am a stir       &
   pressed  redness
    before
    dark                                                    oh
                                                       cherries
       I                                     & I  her knave
   am     so  l  o                    do  am of a valent
   not so very o  my                  you  all in time if
   to say able to tip I  ah   &        o  say  my  little
   creamily o o toes & few   so o  I  any euphoria female  I
    & be muse naked   so can I go o  am of  sweet my fellow I
    for big mouths a  do & on  o  to  you & if   miel   do
   a fat mixing lucky & up oh lip can or bit &  wag it
    paw & but damage is by a synch  be  a   honey do
    paw lip do  all of my mama one it  muses   due here
     a moue I saw her  mime to din or  kissing with
      tulips red pet pale hum in  do  some  us
      so now he is in and her big moment
       I was o we eat  as   rasp  of
       am not I to her    an berry
         me li o toes    o  read
```

Blue Irises

dia

I wanted to mouth you all over
spring clouds spring rain spring
tenderness of afternoons spent
blazing trails to this
place where breath roars through
the famous architecture of a poet's ear
Rose and peony buds and tongue
ichthyous tumble honey and pearl—
the runner's foot has touched and adored
wistaria sprang after you, figs tipped
green air astounded by your passage
to the audient quays of the city
Now it begins, another voyage after nemesis
blue-eyed with the distance of it all

2

I didn't know about this passion

for oh she is also mine

delirium tympanis from the Portuguese

wind in her hair alongside us here

on the deck unhidden she slows your reading down

Fine ground darkness pours into the vessel

beans and flowers adorn the fall—

ichor! ichor! drink to the eyes locked on yours

the mouth that smiles and will speak for itself

I have always done the talking and she

put the words in my mouth saying do melisma

like sunlight be melisma like no sunlight pressed

redness before dark print an iris on her

& do melisma like sunlight astir oh & os etc

3

From the corner of this mouth take

kisses that begin in moonlight

and pitch slow fire over a history of you

reeling in the universe   Rhapsode

you and I have some walking to do, some

stitching together of the story so far, its feat

of silence, of sleeping lightly and listening

for the touch that outstrips all sense

in the hour before dawn   Look we have come

to the walled garden   See how the roses burn!

The lovers in the fountain spoon each other up

their drenched talk stretches the library resources

and when pubis and jawbone snick into place

you face my delight an uncontrollable smile

4

Honeyed learning!   I traced her once

to an island in spring, pointilliste mouse-ear

drifting down the margins   Then she was

phlyctena in the eye of the sea-ear reworking

a disturbance in my name   I found wild choral

allusions and scents that drew a white bee

to not-madness in the folds of her blue gown

This morning the whole world is wet wistaria

battered gutters running and everything drowning drunk

extends a big hand for the reprise

Which comes   Up the road on small trees

is a honey blue inflorescence I can't name

When the gardeners say cyanotis trust your ears

though rain fall into an open mouth

5

She made him a porpoise *gills a-snort*

because it was so hard to configure that body

The words weren't there or they rolled over

and supplied mermaids and mariners   For him

the language is a woman's body and she

will stand out in the rain a hundred years

running it back at him   Hast 'ou seen the rose

in the steeldust (or swansdown ever?)   Have

you seen a falcon stoop?   Hast thou found a nest

softer than cunnus?   Can yee see it brusle

like a Swan?   O so white! O so soft! O so sweet

is she   The sonneteer coughs sneaks

another look at her dolphin scores out

the ellipse after *his vibrant tail*

6

within the temple gate and you knew

she was just delicious cooking up a storm

like this in the big kitchen of your heart

The bee in the fox-glove, the mouth on the nipple

Words! and be forgiven hot kisses translated

with cool accuracy   She ripples past his *lilly*

in a Christal to get at a thyme-burning bee

shut up in a crystalline   Perfect footwork

Bobble down that track loverboy they're bringing

out the focaccia bread studded with olives

and a rough red to match your breathing

She's a contrejour effect on the glittering sea

baby on the breast and a smile that makes your heart stop

Yes we bear sons   They remember milk and honey

7

Blue irises after dark

driving lamplight and Venice-glass

into a fine distraction : *bise* in a crystal line

wanting to know what you know and why

there's a smear of milk on my shirt so long

after weaning these heroes of eros

I planted incendiary kisses on solemn mouths

all over the island of matchless greed

whose trees see and know this and it grows

bees who mistake its name in a line of fire

run to delicate helices where they dance

orientation   Then what is before us

in the night wind where irises calibrate desire

and the rhyme is a voice like sunlight?

honeybee

Apex you'll come to one fine morning

set with that breakfast milk on the island steps

a full feast of fresh air under your belt

It's a small island, turtle in the channel

rare for the latitude, the islanders touchy

about a fragile domestic economy   Two

of them bang away at an extension to the house

dreamed up last night and being paid for

in green dollars   The Friday night pizzas

are legendary if you know which boat to get

and there on the rockface is the aretaloger's sign

sans me fatiguer ni de jour ni de nuit—

a little dairy factory by the name of Isis Lactans

pumping out soft cheeses of a truly divine nature

9

We could all go some more we could go down

for it ourselves and come back on the Cream Run

one quay at a time, mangos bagels wisdom

from the markets where you lean on one elbow

after making love and begin to make

the universe dooby doux to a tune that suits

your ripening sense of history

Going out for the makings, staying in to eat

mouth to mouth, why was it lost most

when we needed that contagion in the telling?

There is still the special place on her head

where they touch her for more of the story

while back in bed a sleep of hands and hearts

is airing nectar in all the generous mouths

How beautiful in jandals, o prince's daughter

the motive bones of your finely dusted feet

on the road to the cape and back

many summers past small clips of paradise

In the dark doorway the Fire Chief, a stir

of silver buttons and a ceremonial axe

as he walks into the picture again   His are the gifts

you are learning to take from the ballerina plate

piled high between you in all of his houses

Sometimes the regalia signifies, sometimes

it's just a couple of beers over lunch

watching your seventeen-year-old self descend

from the tree with the big nest of epiphytic lilies

to where he's waiting saying: Let's go, princess

II

To the north of Paradise a high summer moon

at four in the morning and I call out

the song of your body in the light of what is

before me   I know the precedents I'm looking for

the wise fire of intelligence in a body

that wants to metabolise lightning   I want

to get to the vineyard the river the mountain

the city and the sea undivided by your attentions

then I want to hammer out gamos everywhere

among the beautiful appetising trees of those places

So I get up in the dark and you call   Hey excelsa

your salty shoulder is first, sweet nicotiana next

but most from the open window to this wide bed

white scent from the tree of flowers   And sleep?

Schluck-schluck   perfect mind at work

on perfect body at the confluence of two rivers

called Melilot and Stamp   What a day

it's been salmon in the daypack at four thousand feet

high dives and honeypots into those piscine deeps

and a sweet precision of vocables throughout—

We've got it all as the islanders say, the ins and outs

the ups and downs, the map of the world

on the bedroom floor lost for so long, for so long

passed off as a hand to mouth myth among

painters who travelled the length of the country

to be close to its source   Look, the confluence

of two rivers, the deep relief of the map traversed

hop skip jump and free fall into the art of love

13

Apices that melt you femina climbing

the steps temple days and others minding

children or hanging out the sheets   How

transport is a word among vines—

excelsa and two young roe looking on

Carmel   Who would not forget her clear voice

remaking paradox as the shadow-hunt closes in

on the fabulous slopes of ellipsis:

And I light hearers to you   There she is

swallowed the sun and gives it back

each morning in the bright window *she's there*

on the tip of your tongue her bees working

the red flowers that take you from vine to fire

as she contemplates another shift in the pronouns:

I am the boat of heaven rocking outside

the orbit of the moon and the orbit of the sun

I am the dancer on the plate the one in blue

with a honey stomach full of delectable lies

I am the diver and the baker rolling over

and over in the dry grass which is most like rain

I am the parabola, a crural bow strung

across the single point of my dripping ascent

I am the eater of trees, the drinker of sense

and my name is the crown of a blue eye rising

I learned to write these languages   It is my kiss

on your mouth and there must be no fault

in the transmission   I am before you, I look

after you, I am a slow boat rocking everything

ladies mile

Silence has been important too, pharaoh

gliding through the lips of those who are asleep

Fig crop in my hands, lotus pool in flower

I was in another place when they came to me

and the bright edges of lacunae are seldom torn

by accident   Then fall off the edge of the earth

left hand under my head right embracing me

Why should you wish distance any greater than this?

I am quiet and we are writing in the throat

of all languages   The library at Alexandria burns

but my heart is a pool where the white birds step

among incipient papyri   A world of water

trims a world of fire for Osiris fluid in the blue

and gold of a moment's trust in the driving

Coming home like a derelict Egyptian, changing

worlds, a baby delivered in a jacaranda mist *just*

like mine   The trees are quiet now, the baby grown

and sorrow gone from the place it lay down in

long before I was born   What are we going to do

about that moon in the ngaio tree beating like

a fontanelle?   Can we go on reading the summer

constellations that do not pretend to be literature?

Cicadas   Avocados   But where's that frightening dog

sorrow?   *Lord butterfly on lord hibiscus spray*

are we through crying and the heart's big conversation

with pain?   Two sons, two sons and crowning

isn't a light word any more than a light kiss

resembles a dark one   Which you are

Suppose, sweet eyes, you went into a distant country

mad with the honey and the noon in your throat

a fiery drizzle of rip and glory asking: Where

are the words that broke the heart with beauty?

Not as plains that spread into us slowly, but as

a wind wet with carillons or winter's cold isthmus

in the azure year, you will find the frontiered heart

and write a script of stars across its salt and snow

Birds that think in oceans come and go, their chart

behind their eyes that scarcely sleep   Your mouth's adrift

with ghosts of fire the salt has burned to noontide

blue   Your sweetness ripples through the rain

of a country to which you may never return   You

are the still caesura that breaks a line in two

Leaf, leaf, how can I be sane enough

or mad enough to touch or leave untouched

what silence has to say?   Had I your eyes

your eyes I loved this lifetime, wonder's eyes

and the sun's voice against the nights of eaten moons

would my oppressions be healed?   Sometimes

fighting and dying are better than anything else

Back to the laughter of alien lips and eyes

how shall my heart find home?   I sleep

out of my bones so much bouquet just so much

bite in crystal those cool-dissolving wrists distil

from the sweet landfall water   It is dark

within daylight   The stranger is made of words

that swing by an island's shadow

Smile at that mountain where love was

eaten on a morning when the world held still

in the rain's embrace a promise of iris blue

In the heart every moment a splitting of the moon

in the belly picnics of sky and dancing zephyrs

Be loved be happy, feed and be fattened on this—

A weekend in winter lemon butter thickening

over slow heat, two candy boys ecstatic

on the juicer, Persian mystics on top of the fridge

glinting elevation and excess   Stir and shout

give them (*feet off the green couch right now*) the works!

The parrots of my soul have begun to chew sugar

they turn up the deck and dance loopsville

one in my arms whirled in a golden mirror

Running water you are the phoenician's mouth

lute-curved and eating his dreams like flame

I have lost the light of your laughter very cool

and sweet the breath of limes or an aureole

of waters falling where a hand might cup the breast

of one who like the young moon is white

and strange and slender   The gleaming human

lamp on your mad ship's shoulder is a woman

drawn up by the fine chain of silence white

and unbroken about her neck   Her full breast

pours out a mirth of stars, bright areolae

or glittering revolution in heaven's cool

breathing of lines which set the double-curved flame

of the lover sea against her laughing mouth

Jewelling, or if the Silenced laugh

memory from the wheel of white stars turning

against the sky, what should the thought of my heart

do but flood out the empty heavens?   These were

my children, my beloved   Take them, hold them forever

as you held them first, small bodies motive

in a sea of air and learning the warm animal

from us all walking in the houses of the sun

Lifts, utter mirror of his hand on the wheel

the strategy of repeats that still gesture him

live in a world filling with the tears of Isis

We have been sad too long   Close up this desolate

house and drive to where the island's wet light

candours the moon on the river wider than a smile

Keeping Warm

you there at
the long end
of my arm

drive me to
work & back
over the bridge

to distraction
icecreams in
the wind or

moon on the
beach : *them*
dauphins

berserk about
us on their
offshore roads

razzle dazzle
moonlight
climb up the

near side of
heaven's cloudy
smile : this is

heaven & you
in it following
la vie dansante

warm rowdy
voice reading
to the kids

draped word
perfect about
you doing

equal parts
charm & need
for me looking

on decoding
nuance (oh
clouds) the house

needs a paint
the Saturday
skilsaws howl

into September
& cups of tea
punctuate the

hard questions
: there was a
moment when

that look in
your eye closed
all distances

ka-boom as
the poets say
dreamily

two people
get together
like *spring*

and *moon*
time & place
fold around

them : yes
there's specific
moonlight and

a curve in
the road where
it takes your

breath away
this is local
right here up

close & it's
your bridge to
where I stand

laughing at
it already
written in

big glittering
letters : let's
go out there

& do the poem

as far as i can see

dove

persephatta

swimming in the black river a tale emerges

twists and turns about her sometimes urgent

sometimes mirror blank   she doesn't play

lazy riverine though the water lip laps

surfaces and resumes such talk along her flanks

that strength runs out as need walks in

riparian parties onto the wintery tombolo

river I put my trust in plum blossom words

dragged under leaving no language safe

from itself   a girl going to meet her mother

is abducted marries death fixes destruction

in her own image   the script has lashed her

to sufficiency and reticence those broken limbs

in the current she steps from wholly diffident

persicifolia

and with rescues to effect   *peachleaved nymph*

sorrowing (are you sorrowing?) on the waters

bearing you to heaven's presumptuous grin

mock pursuits and marriage beds collapse the letter

space where a diction hides her people   bride fly out

of his hand who wades the Money Pool at sunset

and stumbles across the aporia at dawn singing

heaven is here in a kiss   gifts of prophecy and healing

pucker the valley of that leaf you copied

to the body in perpetuity   your mouth is leaves

on his face nymphæ peachleaf bride

of loops and costume change swirling cerulean

in the stream a blue lotus a white lotus vanishing

bride peachleaf nymphæ   your mouth leaves

persica

his face a court of angels upriver

twelve dynasties east and drumming the morning star

into the arms of the sun   your *ha* is an almond in flower

above the heart that hears his *hu* and is unbound

uproarious with æons going past in a shout

a shimmy on the grape ropes a ripple up the pool

beholder to beggar to pleader please

walk with me here in the spring   there is no foot

can be imagined without its wing no convention

without the literal honey the literal where

and when and how the literal sleeps as on a body

of water solely its coeval estimate of drift

Angelike   *where* twelve twelves with wings

upraise another hungry drummer of spring

persienne

ah persienne   the wind takes my breath away

I see it over the blue islands laughing like six children

looking out to sea   their voices rise higher and higher

their mountain is the bellied sail taking them now

to meet everything that was wished   in the printed folds

rivers of air gardens of wind and the sea-going craft

drawn up near the place they have called Paradise

ah persienne   breathless they reassign what is given

I was asleep dreaming in a dark place   it pressed

on me and I was afraid   the weeping dove was lost

to the sea roads the air gardens had forgotten her

deft play about the topsails   it is recalled

by the high voices in their eagerness to be

embarked *this dear morning* into the outward

perse

spray of blossom whiter than oceans

jumping together over the reef run wild

into the sea   *I go to libraries*

because they are the ocean the spray of blossom

she is bending passion *a wavecrest* mountaineer

of the word and the body which reads *Everest*

floating like that like a summer's night resolved

a glitter in the long hazy dawn   and dove

among the waves at last herself morning

and evening star but one body *I   not my eyes*

reading day in day out the little distance

carried forward by the jacaranda in bloom

over the gate and the foot jubilant in kicking

its elemental doubts into the sky *per se*

hesperides

dolce

oranges seem to grow wild in the bay that is *cloud*
carried by the wind   there my boys swim out
of the easterly blow *Haukapua* they shout
the huff and the hook the kick and the splash
the green bay is full of their golden bodies   persistent
ungentle the wind rides overhead as they trail back
for showers by the open window a towel on the pillow
sweet rhythms of the bach where they wake and sleep
to arithmetical Variations on shelter and a doorway
the performance of the sun at noon a memory printing
windmills under the canopy of leaves   *highly aromatic*
days of no event but virtuoso growth how tall
they are how straight of limb what storms of noise
the keyboards take to be sure the game proceeds

getting away

angel wings beating harder than ever light drumming
on skinny shoulders pertinent to select displays of
temper and charm   it was always important to knock
with your elbow a dozen beer smoked kahawai something
to put on the table   then to wear as little as possible
as long as possible to eat late sleep lots and sit around
talking in the dark remembering *the buzzing of the bees*
in the lemonade trees looking over at Paku so built up
big rock candy mountain on its estuary of song
hurricane surf that had to be swum hand in hand
under skies blue enough to discreate a cyclone
there is white sand mile after mile in loneliness
and crushed shells giving it a border of violet
we stop later for the golden oysters of Miranda

a nautilus

I put the children to bed and go out
hunting the ancestors   the one who is afraid
of the night adrift up there in his deep blue covers
the one who will curl between us so quietly
nobody wakes and he is safe   I have left them again
unable to sleep and knowing their sleeping
is my return *to the wide nets washing out in moonlight*
they stir as the house gears down they call out
as I pass I call back I am there when they stagger about
to gulp water and pee   they lock the doors I left open
and skim up ladders in their sleep   I need them
they prevent my disappearance from the world
they bring me back howling overacting for my blurred
attention the cradle boat drawn out on the falling tide

staying put

the girl on the fridge found her walled-up skin
but won't be without her magnetic babes   they frolic
around her a sea of alphabetic cries AzGVw sLKƎ
yY hSPr fLOOp low on the feminine with a modicum
of consonantal drift *you get the picture* we get
the picture thrown around and stuck back *baby baby*
my sINGER Flips her fishy tail   *Mistakes I know*
I've made a few the impossible back-arch her attempts
at keeping it all up in the air *Citrus limetia* rare and interesting
though worthless a horticultural curiosity   which version
do you want three commas and a dash or four ellipses
following a special form of berry yes a *hesperidium*
what could be kept separate was never worth the bother
only human now she flippers every little morph

dulce

the Nuyoricans went to Piano Beach and found tai tāne
unbelievably gentle   the messages were adjuncts
to their honeymoon performed in blacksand with a bag
of hot plums and a modesty of towels   we clapped
the lipsticks untwirling on the front veranda at home
we waited for the remembered fragrance and we listened
for the old motors overhead in the long light evening
candy I call my sugar candy and the letters he wrote her
persist with orangeblossom snipped from the ivory lace
of her panniers   *don't forget to change your flying boots*
she wrote him on the invitation thinking maybe
of this frangipani coming into flower on the porch
most admired veranda and of the hesper ride
his DC-3 still charters for our collaborating hearts

torches

song

twenty three and a half
degrees unstoppered
in the night garden to which
your lips are scripture
and ecliptic tilt in one
flamboyant kiss   curse
her who with half a head
twenty three and a half
degrees celestial sought
among these one moment
in arrest forgetting the stop
put to the garden
as it bumped us and time
stood entreatied in your face

dark torch

hey old flame   I swam
across the harbour just to buy you
some shoes   all night all night
in the water howling songs
uncontained publications of love
with a flea in its ear and its pants
on fire   fool! liar!
(waves arms) who am I to hold
a dark torch up to heaven
and the ferry's disappearing lights
I didn't have the boat fare
but I knew the fit of your feet
and the extraordinary hours kept
in that boutique   I swim aflame

one

sunny thank you for the
billowing parachute
silk April wave
April morning winning
the fit of the hand
to the falls the sonnets
the lips retouched
the shell I am holding
sunny one so blue
in this place between
conquering surfaces
each word I flew
was its vanishing point
out on the alba sea

walking on air

two good ones
rolling over and over
one so loving
the other they change
places alternate
days turning the sky
cap of darkness
cap of daylight starry
retinue of sparrows
answering the sailors'
prayer Dioscuri
boys infrangible
gems how
is a bird's wing?

what is

it might be very early
it might be very late
fleecy marble the world
curve sticks out of
love's proper sphere
at the feet of the rider
stolen away for love
smoke touches the square
of the winged horse
and the lightfield explodes
blue flame and white
one handstand
for love stolen away
from the sooty altars

from a woman, a rose, and what has it to do
with her or they with one another?

I

Do you see me? I am falling out of a blue sky where my days were as dancers in a maze, sure-footed and smiling. I stood in my garden pulling loquats off the tree and eating them to be full of spring. I filled up on summer and kept the city busy with correspondence. Flightpaths criss-crossed at my feet, bees fizzed and joy was my middle name.

Then a pair of taxis went head to head in a distant country so suddenly I didn't see the difference but it was a wide white threshold. When I couldn't thread a needle, when I could no longer see the faces of my children or trim their nails, when the colour of money disappeared (and I bareheaded in the midday sun) then falling began and I cried out against it. What's one wing beating time on the steel drum of the sky? What is the sight of my eyes to the great oratory of the labyrinth?

There was a send-off, they gave me flowers and asked where I would go. To open the eyes of the soul, I said. Good wishes hovered over the gathering and messages flew into my pockets. There is a way, I said, but this is only the first gate. I give what is left of the light of my eyes, I have fallen out of a clear sky.

2

How will you know me? My signs were set in heaven but they are lost. If I was ever the moon's daughter that name is gone too. I am the daughter of the widow's son, eldest daughter of an eldest son, eldest child of an eldest child. I am the daughter of the widow's child, eldest child of an only daughter, eldest daughter of the youngest child. Eldest son and youngest daughter, eldest and youngest of the widow women before and after the war, married on the first day of spring in a small mountain town.

The children built a house on the mountain. The children built a house by the sea. Their children were born and played there, they could tell you about the lino patterns or the plates driven around the kitchen at speed. They cooked salt dough in the stove on the bank and pulled out real fragrance for history. They remember hurt skin around the mouth stuck with blue gum that wouldn't come off. See them laugh, see them play. See Sweetie run.

But the widows' children died and were at last a white sift on the air of a mountain gully. I told their stories to my children, I made them live in the eyes of my sons, I watched the stories grow up by other shorelines, below other mountains.

I am not a daughter now and I cannot see my sons though I know they see me. This is the gate of tears, another farewell. Beyond it an aqueous humour prevails and we may swim, but not as once on a morning by the raft in a sea of flowers. Here I give up my dear ones.

4

Where did we get to? There was a hot sweet time (and tears and thunder) then marrying.
The jasmine showers down, the star jasmine in its rich drifts, impossible to say how long
or where next. My dress was the sky looking east over a harbour at sunset, indigo reaching
for rose, all my days sheer pearl in the height before darkness. There was sojourning here
a first time, sojourning here a second, one moment, for ever. There is never leaving and
leaving all the time.

It's nightfall. On the waterfront the folks are throwing shoes and rice, big reception for
the moon coming up, little black dog dancing and music in the air like water near the
mark. Everything is served in a *jus*, nectar and all the games to be played. The car pulls up
with its tin cans, there's some hooting and carrying on, the big acceleration then well-
wishers drift back to the party on the beach.

We push and we pull and the shapes of the world are accommodated. Next morning
there's a spring to renew the zonule in. Roses swing, dog barks. If touch is a torch and the
difference still you, can it matter so very much if I do not see your face? I hold you, I kiss
you. How can I go on without you? The price of the gate is too high, it tears me apart and
I am afraid.

ice

snow feathers down gentle gentle injurious whispers *sleep and forget* kiss kiss and the roof of the world collapses compacted whispers *forget* the icecave with its jewelled snake, hiss of blades on the frozen lake, ridge of the six glaciers rehearsing the shouts of dancers *forget* revelry stillness love the snow walk where I heard train call mountain from mountain working up and down the spirals in the high passes. My hands curled in their pockets, dead obedient daughters, sleepers under the river, sleepers under the lake.

I took off my jewellery and gave it to a stranger in a tea house saying *Bow Lake holds the tears I couldn't keep; Bow River is my voice above sorrow.* The silver blackened as it cooled against the snow and disappeared perhaps not forever. I could hear it between footfalls in the stranger's bag as he started back along the lake. It was the sound of running water. It was light honey on the wind below the pass. *Listen for my voice. Touch my wet face.* Bring me where panic has gone out of the world.

stone

I was hung on a hook three days and three nights, a corpse among corpses in the palace of disaster. I saw nothing, heard nothing, was nothing. Only this : through the lid of one eye a small song, crept under the doors of stone, capers before her who was me. Now there are two singing who lift the heavy lids of her eyes which are mine. Closer they come to the lady unloved in her hours of pain as she walking above was ever attended by joy. They stroke her temples, touch her ears, take her hands and ride with her over the jagged plain. There is blood in the bed and soon a child's head crowning between her legs.

As she who is me allows herself to be touched by their couvade, a spring begins in the rock. When she who was me asks what gift can be made for their gift they ask for the body on the wall. She looks at it, white flowers opening head to foot, and gives her assent. Quickly the strangers remove their effigy and carry it away, calling the stations of the journey as they go. Oils and tears complete the work and when they reach the surface there is no cortège, only a child crying in the night and one who brings comfort to it.

You brought me here, I (a stranger) sang the release of sorrows borne from one depth to another height. We came out of the dark loving.

milk & honey

wilderness

I hope I'm not disturbing you
fellow traveller
renamed Constant and much taken
by revolutionary copy writing
on the outskirts of my
dream that you are dead

soon I'll walk from the wreckage
carrying a small case of smoking documents
no more diamond body no wild goose
this is what was left after the explosion
I'll open my hand and show you a heart
like a black sun on the other side of time
and I'll walk out of here soon

atman I breathe
and the light shatters

faith and rage

chaosmos 1

I'm sick and it's the end of the century   beat
lack little of dying
and only the contents of this plastic bottle
are propping me up
this morning
I forgot to put on my clothes   the crease defers
here I am on the boat   Venus Magnolia
with a bag packed for running away
with 500 ml of arano
no preservatives
with a camisole because it's hot   peau de soie
with something in my pocket   via spica
written by you or me
if this was the workers' boat
the suits would be snooping about
my elbows would be in   impulsive behaviour
I'd be focused
I wouldn't be spread out
scrawling ignoring the future
I'd be forgetting the
poem the sheets my used-up arms and legs
I'd be ok
without you
where you are 1 am   moonlight on a lost river

      in the private room I'm dancing

      into the decline of the century
      strictly informal, the walls glissade
      no designs on me, no shirt
      black toreadors
      and a beaten necklace
      making little steps closer to

The Spiritual In Art
I'm so smooth
in profile, arms open for the abrazo
bailing out of this system
of notation into the abstract
and for eleven minutes
you were there in the band
but you had gone
outside the theatre is a riot
but I'm lost in the wings
are you coming back
by cab to pick me up
is this the start I'm looking for?

chaosmos 2

someone bungies from the centre span   public address
next morning on the same boat
perhaps it's an election stunt
the passengers say
squinting up the harbour   o vividence
I'm feeling better
in the bag is a book and a broken umbrella
this way as well as that
decussation seems to be complete   XX
it's still hot   one candela
in my swansdown boundaries
and the year of the world sails on
we explained it once
a moon egg thrown between the legs
of a woman on a birthing stool
one tough egg on a lunar drop
dipping the surface

of the waves
trying to get a sense of how
being in both places
is silk and some words on a page

beating like a fontanelle

mi amiga

this

is the kiss
that forgets
the kiss
that goes
before
the kiss
that was never
the kiss
after
the kiss
that started
the kiss
that folds
the kiss
that touches
the kiss
that kisses
your lips

chaosmos 3

it's howling from the north
I am living and dying   see BE
in the ruins of an Indus word
for breathing
every morning the boat travels
towards a luminal horizon
every night it docks in a new part   fiorello rossi
of the stack   walks upstairs
take another funny story out
of the wind's mouth
blow me forgetfulness
blow me a particle moving
through my languages   am art is are
through my lovely oblivion   was were would
let me remember   become
my stemma my sleep   in the wind
what you put in my mouth   delusory waivers
when we are being   there is
moist osmosis most
how am I here I am   here
torn top vitamin C resurgent   a choir
moving around   (something)
circling about   (something)
as an egg dropped out of the moon
every word remembers   limbs again
every pain replicated   folds again
I remember pain
so deep in the folds
I forget myself   renounce that booty
lunge through the opening   again and again
caught seized bootied   neglected
I am forgetful   full with that apprehension I send from myself

there's a pearl and a diamond

one of them is mine
the other you gave me
as I went out in the world
I set the stone
close to the bubble
and they never left off
talking rubbing glistening
they are the surface
of the seas you fly over
going into the morning
of a new world
and somewhere down there
is a votive figure
cunt like a pomegranate
blue mako clit
she has the diamond in her teeth
the pearl in her mouth
she is you
she is me
flying into the sun
naked with you
nacre with me
this is how we come
into the new world
diamond and pearl
under the tongue
these are the distances
petite fille
make them gleam
put them into my mouth
and jet yourself
into the space between
your lips and mine

tourbillon 1

amnesiac I return without sound
looking for the trace
that knows my name   beon
low morning sun does something
to the coffee smoke   materialises
black weave of print or wool
almost the lobe of *l'aube*   almost the scent of a bee
or the painted nipples sucked hard
and squirting rosewater
full of pectin full of petals, the parallel
world is a mouth mapping
amplitude a bubbling world
burst open one day in the city
aqueous nacreous bee bonnet
making the wheel of the sun go round   circumambient
locating me in the house I build
the curtains I draw the bed I make
the knife I throw into your heart
an electuary stunt
because I am thinking brocades
and white waterfalls of being
because the coffee hisses
over hot steel and is not what it seems
the white flowers fall   it's autumn
the weave undreams itself
I can't stop loving you   I've made up my mind
we will build this house every morning
with arms wide we say ambient
a hive of industry
what we do   and do not do
being both   being both
going round this being   being

in the house of ourselves its smoke   s
and the hiss of its new conception
be both be both be both
the covering of my rage by water
the setting of doves on that water   but first the storm

                    I tell you we live

                    stratospread on pillows
                    where absence never was
                    the plug-ins download for free
                    and we redesign each other
                    in the first language of obedience
                    I ask you to believe me
                    and you say you do

tourbillon 2

the words go liquid   cells uncapped
sea breaking at the end of the road
tells me how near
the composite noun gets
to its cochleal adventure
behind screens of pittosporum
and the grapevine dying off now
we have been Amphiscians here
inhabitants of tropics whose shadows
fall at one time northward
at another time south
shadow *skia* amphi *both*
both-shadows *amphiscii* the load
shifts and the eyes skip *ii*
over the great ocean of Kiwa

blowing across the mouth of the amphora   amphoric
kissing the waves the skin of the ocean   Kiritai
driven onshore by low pressure systems
circling like galaxies
historical consciousness
or prayer wheels kicking round
a new dimension of the sacred   a keen lexical ear
because the eyes don't work
and she rages in outer darkness   aorist in the making
trying to run the border
caught in the wild waves and the birth
that floated the child in kelp
they said was her hair
lost horizon, simple, without limit
to the north and to the south   how is a bird's wing?

    event / orison

    one two three
    and you were speaking
    it was the first part
    of a poem or a voyage
    it was a map
    and your lips moved
    behind my ear
    before my eyes
    in a dance or a play
    with the striped gold headcloth
    that ties at the back
    like a shell from the scallop beds
    of Alexandria
    yes
    Jimmy and Kosta and Angelo

in the kitchen
as you move to the door
two quick kisses and a lingering
indispensable
a shadow and a play
going on into the light
of day *how beautiful*
you are waiting in the vestibule
with sealed orders
for holding up the sky

tourbillon 3

aorist, heart
what is this road we are on?
freedom of risk in that excellence   aristeia
at the extreme edge of
human possibility
sweet pulp under my tongue
in the comfortable life
aorist, breathe
show me where I must go
the limitations of other
past tenses melt into darkness
undefined and therefore free
among others
her attributes are the dolphin   lipwrap
the dove the swan the pomegranate   annealing
and the lime tree   in the oven of the world
but even she in her loveliness
could be the next suicide bomber   among others
working deeper and deeper   tessella

into the cave lined with explosives   tessella
is it the heart? I don't know
even she in her loveliness
bottom of the throat   top of the ladder
eleventh of anything   second nature
even she a.o.
may come whirring out of the sky
too late, even she   exotic matter
can only second-guess
curved time
and find the book, and send it
sealed with equatorial spills
towards the light

          we are fully linguistic

          dissolved
          into free speech
          in two minds at once
          travelling light
          into the light
          You are my soul
          I am your body
          the enigma
          of the perfect form
          no signs left
          tongues on fire
          with the words
          of angels
          the fiction
          is All or Nothing
          all is
          too much

nothing is
too much
I have come from Babylon
I have come to Babylon
I dreamed my love
I loved my dream
O Sister
in this city of canals
where I AM
I like sitting in the park
when everything
holds its breath
at the moment
it gets dark
when
the Stranger lights
a match
and
says
Welcome . . .

cairo vessel 1

Girl
night and day you are the One
        I lie awake till dawn   dreaming
only you beneath the moon
        and under the sun
you make my heart into a drumbeat
        stretched over the morning sky
I hear your voice and I'm gone
        all-of-me and forever   fastpost
I know how to pick you up
        if you'll just let me kneel down
nobody else in my heart but you
        nobody in yours
        but me

I want you
        like fat and honey
you are fine linen on the bodies of the grandees
        white raiment on the bodies of the gods
you're incense at the nostril of Always
        oils from the lip of As If
you are the finger putting on my seal-ring
        and he who turns it at will
you are mandrakes in the hand of God
        a date-cake dipped in honey
        lilies set by bread
love comes tripping up and down the river
        all the days of our lives
love is a steamboat ticket
        to anywhere you want to go
we'll be together
        day in day out I'll give you kisses
if we have to be old
        let's laugh like candied hippos
        up to our ears in mud

my god my lotus
       my blue water lily
riding with the north wind
       across the Lake of Myrrh
gentle your fingers in my hair
       your sweet breath behind my ear
blossoms float past us
       we're part of a galaxy that whirls
I want to put on sheer linen
       and go down to the river to bathe
walking a little ahead   knowing
       you're picking up the vapour trail
I'm your spice girl   I make everything
       all right

come on   follow me
       to the pool with its fringe of reeds
I'll go down into the water with you
       I'll come out with a red carp
       wriggling on my fingers
here it is my warrior of the beautiful weapons
       look at it and look at me
       looking at you   we should kiss

Boy
little sister you're on the far bank
       and the river swirls between us
it's pulling me into the floodwaters
       and a crocodile grins on the sandbank
I wade right into the torrent
       I'm thinking about you so close so far
the crocodile's just a handbag
       I zip him up and walk on those waters
       like a miracle man

your hot love makes this possible
        your water-spell is irresistible
I see the darling of my heart
        waiting faraway so close
        I can't take my eyes off you

now we're together my heart bangs
        I open my arms and you walk right in
my heart is happy   can't you feel it jump
        like a fish in a lotus pool?
the night goes on and on
        since you came to save me sweetheart

when I get you close your beautiful arms
        go around me like a princess fresh
        from Punt
you're all Missy-plant and fragrant pomades
        bundled up just for me

I kiss your lips open
        drunk on your intoxicating mouth
tell me you're having a good time
        goddess   tell me the drug works
in your heart-depths too
        as we think about a room for the night
I asked the temple girls for advice
        they said If she's your queen
        set fine linen around her body
        lay on scented white sheets
        and a whole forest of moth-orchids
you are my queen and your limbs are sails
        that take us to This
        drenched in the oils of love

cairo vessel 2

Boy
I wish I were her pizza boy
      always on the end of a string
hey I'd bring mandrakes and lilies
      hand-delivered to her room in a jar
she'd sniff them dreamily
      and offer me all the delights of her body

I wish I were washing out her clothes
      even for just one minute
I'd be so happy just to handle
      filmy linen that had touched her body
I'd wash out the musky sweetness
      that clings to her underthings
I'd wipe my body with that party dress
      she wore yesterday to the lagoon
my joy would be complete
      ecstasy would carry me away

I wish I were that cute ring
      wrapped around her little finger
I'd feel her love
      every single day
I'd be close enough
      to steal her heart away
I wish I had all the mornings of the world
      to sit and look at her
if I could be her mirror
      this gaze would be unending
I'd be over the moon
      showing her beautiful face
to the world
      and adoring every move she makes

little sister every day I want you
   like frangipanis and the lemon tree
   in blossom
the sun is high I shake your branches
   and white stars fall on me *holà*
Mebebs flourish Ir-trees burst into bloom
   the stone-blue flower and the mandrakes
   send out their dreamy magic
fennel runs wild ginger festoons the paths
   hibiscus butterflies unfold everywhere
life expands
   when you're here with your spice garden
and your tropical ricochets
   let's drink birthday wine

I wish I'd been the first
   to see her blue eyes open wide
I'd do anything to keep my baby doll
   happy and here with me
why would she ever go?
   I'm the best on the block
I bring her pashtoons
in the morning and lunations
late at night she giggles and lets me in
   with my bread and puppet show
I'm in a spin and so is she
   that's how it works with us

I'm dizzy we've been in bed all day
   sun swinging around us
like a camera on a trolley
   she had to run to the wharf
to catch her boat
   in a cloud of butterflies
   and off the shoulder kisses

she's banished every evil from my body
            I won't wash for a week
I want to smell of her so everyone knows
            what we've been up to
and the torment I'm going through
            because I'm in public view
when I should be wrapped around her
            world without end *amen*

I went to the beach
            where her boat sailed at sundown
I'd spent the night in pain
            unsure life could continue
what did I see but the sun rising
            on a heart moulded in sand
white shells for butterflies
            pressed into its beautiful curves

she's banished every evil from my body
            I'm in orbit around her
I won't stop singing
            I won't start washing
I won't [finish this line]
            until we're together again

ODM 1266 + O CAIRO CGC 25218

future song

birds are falling out of the plum trees

totally drunk on juice

we might go north

for a few days
to a neighbour's bach on the Hokianga
or we might not

éloignement

the luxury
of going along making it up

or not even moving
at all

this is the house of air

anyone can knock on its yellow door
and find the festival in full swing
meaning getting ready meaning filling up
meaning shaking out the sheets
and making room in the fridge   oh the calls
come in and we take them one at a time
happiness grief pain of losing
what we counted on the blue-flowered tree
over the gate, ourselves dansants
under its summer-moving boughs
the linden dream and the hats we brought home
in the script we were sure of
will still be sure of but differently now

the house is full of music and words, everything
we danced to everything we ever sang or stole
and brought out later under the feathery tree
where the picnic baskets wait

a painting walks into the house on Christmas day

it's eight feet tall, a gift
from one to the others who find in it
islands waterfalls maps and genetic scribble
but most of all fractals of love
will we be old? we don't know
we might see bougainvillea
on a valley road and be reminded
of missions gone back
to wilderness and ourselves
a stain spreading into a lost picture

new year

the dove
wakes me
each day

koo
koo
koo
koo-roogh

the lilies
jig in their
white skirts

on one
silver foot
the teapot

on one
silver foot
the adept

the silk tree
over the stone wall

on the other side
a book and

goldeneyed
the wine
of the estate

the plums
the avocados
the corn

I rescue you
you rescue me
koo koo koo
koo-roogh

one silver foot

somewhere in the hills

is a fountain splashing down stone steps
it's called Fonte Fria, the cold spring
we might go to see it
or we might not

éloigné

it will be there for us
or it will not

I leave plenty of gaps
because this is a future song
the fountain writes on the wind
we will see it
or else we will not

I make a momentous guess
and write *fado*

if I don't see you again
these footsteps will show you the way

journey to portugal

the words

take me down
into the sea
Viagem a Portugal
concrete steps
ankle-deep
in white roses
Largo da Portagem
where the boats
tie up below
a saint inside
a silver tomb
on Alcáçova hill

I like everything that's real
And everything that's right

verde, verde, verde

we walk in a jardim botânico first
to a fountain with four gates
and cardinals in a procession   doves roll
over the white paths and water splashes
in the centre of the mata
then we ascend to the terrace and read
under a tree so big it could be
the carousel of the world going round
dropping messages that extend
the day of words and make us jump
into space when we thought
we were safely on the ground

verde, verde

words beginning the restoration
of what lives forever
one day apart   half-moon over
the celebrating city   victory
over death   the bells ringing out
shocked intoxicant   the young green wine
bubbling like sunlight
in a fountain   água / sol / água
children troop past with notebooks
we set our clocks to local time

verde

how many times do we come to the fountain?
how many times do we drink?
how many signs and how many angels
and the sun coming up in geminate?
he reads and the words go over my head
he sings and the water falls on me
it happens here and it happens to us
he shares what he has given away

saudade, saudade, saudade

when I write it comes out one way
when I sing it's a different language
long shadow fingers holding the page
palavras the words   fruits and flowers
dropping through the filtered light
little horses of the carousel
remaking corporeal existence
the aqueduct calls out its transparent name
and the doves roll over *roll over*
the white path the stone steps the fountain
of the saints in their sandals of gold

Funerals of King Cheops in old gold and Me!

she counts ten angels

on the sarcophagus
behind the poets reading
in the biblioteca on the hill
I remember and I have looked
for the ugliest one of all
smiling white weight of a cobblestone
in one pocket   empty box of stars
in another   and mixed together the dust
of the two realities falls   *white and black gold*
on my fingers   adoration dancing

And all this spring landscape is the moon above the fair,
And all the fair with noises and lights is the floor of this sunny day

a poet from New York hammers
on the library door   another walks
towards the locked cabinets
with a camera that catches the sound
of bats high up in the vault
and an oculos lifting off for heaven
the indigenes have come to listen
but like us they want to photograph
the gold and guarded books
in natural light   a giant apple fills
one viewing platform
Fernandinho with his little flowers
another   was it enough
to get the curtains drawn back?
to have the master narrative
blink and shift on its haunches?

the gold is beautiful   it listens
to words free as lepidoptera
in a rain forest   it calls notes
from the harpsichord
that make us forget to breathe

each day we eat at the long tables
of the Cafe Justiça e Paz
house red is our drink
white paper the linen where we draw
maps and tributary street plans
showing each other
the old town running down
into its republican places   and rough
translations of the river gliding by
dos Poetas

at night among the ruins
we imagine waiting for the barbarians
two hundred years of anxiety
listening to their dogs in a campo
beyond the walls   scratching
soft Xs into the night by columns
like broken molars around a peristyle
who's fooled?   we know it's us
looking west towards the past
that is to be   we are in Portugal
facing the sea and talking
to the Lusitani

My soul shattered like an empty vase.

domingo

down the Rua dos Espirals
with its honeysuckle its wistaria
its datura trees hanging over the wall
to the parque (this is easy) and discover
a mirror of the new world
held up to reality in the ruins
of the old   we've stumbled on Brazil
in a forest of exotic birds and vistas
through the trees   is this the shape
of all we are?   the double staircase
the mirrors either side of a mossy fountain
built to look like a waterfall   at its foot
someone empties a fish into a pool
squeezing it to start an inundation
fingers behind the gills of the world fish
or spilling out a river of stars
a monster or a guardian   we can't tell
but we've seen them both before
and water rushing through
making its cobbly noise, its river spirals

we make our way up Rua dos Confusos
past the cats of the students in their
dingy republicas   *I've always been confused*
as if it's yesterday I hear you
the first aria hits the hot pavement
we climb to the top of the hill
two butterflies en pointe
settling on the nose of Dom Dinis
borboletas butterflies *maravilhas* marvels
we go to the palace at noon
and eat a banquet with many courses
in honour of the Excelentíssimo Senhor
whose blue spires brought us here
we go to the chapel and hear

folk singing with wooden adufes
from Idanha-A-Nova and a man
with an oxcart on a pole
carrying the bride to her wedding

that night is formed in a sidewalk cafe
Borboletas Maravilhosas
the Ladies' Anarchist Internet Choir

Reality, come back tomorrow.

house of the fountains

there never was a view
we couldn't improve   all it took
was a word   grapevine   wrought iron
whispering in the Cloister of Silence
which century whose history
can we go now   under the trees
drinking coffee and scribbling furiously
on a black and white guitarra
I know what to do
and it's true we get to the ruínas
without difficulty   and it's Galicia
it's Arles it's fields of composition
the siren at one o'clock   it's almoço
step and step   everything will happen
mosaics the colour of hyacinths
flicking like a gecko's tongue
fountains buried fifteen hundred years
playing in rows on pools with gardens
set like barges on a lake   spigots
pouring that curtain of noise
off the water truck
in summer   *how did they do that?*
how did the tree sail like a ship?   everything
with its feet in water   everything
floating in air   the bells ring two o'clock
we leave to get lost in the hills
the gorges the cascades the river
crossing and re-crossing a meander
we don't know where we're going
step and step   the bells ring across fields

cut for hay near olive trees
out of a plein air fantasy   the long way
to Luso   *step and step and step*
to the enchanted forest and its grottos
sanitários next to the ravine   *step and step*
the armillary sphere with its bracelets
flashing in the late sun   the swan
pure Manuelino and the loggia
where wistaria trails us again
a terrace with a view of the next millennium
in the dreaming arms of the last
all circles of a single sphere
step and step and step   to the pool
no magnolia fringe
water splashing from a plastic pipe
hand-lettered notices on rocks
painted white *No Washing in the Fountain*
two swans sailing nearby
No Picking of Floras and Ramagens
one black one white
the stone ploomps once and is gone
step and step and step   ten pools ascending
each with its black and white game
of contemplation in the forest   the double
stair of what we are   walking up
with heavy steps then down
one either side   counting out loud
each pool different   each flight
part of a single prayer *anglesite* the host
stationed and holding its breath

a little cave at the top and the spring
rising without ceremony
a Triton holding open the dolphin's maw
and nereids like fireboats
rejoicing in the Place of the Restoration
step and step and step   the Place of Ripples
stretching into the distance *extasiado*
but we are still here in the park   free
to walk or to look through the grilles
of the Via Crucis chapels at terracotta scenes
almost lifesize   *the night in the wilderness*
or the terrace with its far-reaching view
under the Navigator's tower
and azulejo romance on the walls
see, she's put a flower in his flying helmet
for love as they teeter above a lily pool
then a barco full of devils before or after
O Novo Mundo   delirium with open breast
beside him and confidence to burn
the bells ring seven o'clock   the sun
descending   a dance on the terraço
due west   a passage   a festival
two who love each other driving away
with the sun in their eyes   *step and step*
to the ruins of the fire   on a run
for the setting sun plunging into the sea

The language is a block of marble.
OH, TO RELIVE THE SORROW.

mirabile dictu

work for the living

one by one they come out
the piece of paper with the poem transcribed
at five in the morning and folded
into the driver's pocket
another with the words of the song
the Yorkshireman doesn't need
he's brought cucumbers from his garden
she found pūriri around the corner
I'm looking up the Latin for *big flower*
or maybe *really big flower*
and pulling it from the tree

too many funerals but the road
is clear to the north   the driver
puts his foot down
the words in his pocket speed
the conversation the weave of
bad singing bad hearing bad eyes
stopping only for a bad joke
across the road from the Hundertwasser
toilets   *they call me mellow yellow*
the tourist train rolls up the main street
someone takes a picture on a phone
stories flash by   Ruapekapeka Ōhaeawai
Culloden the Spanish Armada
the wars the families deaths and clearances

at Te Kotahitanga we find him
whose words have brought us
to the north   *wheear 'ast ta bin sin'*
ah saw thee   he asks silently
did you clean up the shattered teacup
the milk spilling onto the floor?
the Lake Poet walks in trailing clouds
the Persian Ecstatic takes a spin

around the room and King James
does benison in both languages
body and soul   light and air
pūriri grieves and the Really Big Flower
opens its lemon soap heart   *Ephphatha!*
the birds in the trees are suddenly uproarious
and then we hear rain outside

it's gone by the time
we emerge and the van has him
safely on the road to Wharepaepae
we are slower getting up there
the carter on the horizon calls out
in the arms of the road   a translation
anyone might understand
replying to the voice in the wind
as the old lady opens her arms
and takes him into the earth

lost children
and talk that goes on into the night
around a table in a house on another hilltop
where an old friend pulls out the first book
and inside it another piece of paper
with a handwritten poem she reads
remembering where it came from
taking the path between that coast
and the travellers she is feeding tonight
the cucumbers went into the salad
more books more history more wine
the driver's poem is unfolded
as a full moon gets up over the valley
A red libation to your good memory, friend.
There's work yet, for the living.
in the morning a bird will call from the trees

visible invisible   riro she explains
to the man without a hat who knows
the song but can't sing it now
to save his life   riroriro little stranger
the wars the deaths the clearances
one who intrudes into my shadow
I don't recognise shadows   his face
a translation anyone might understand

mirabile dictu

imagine   the world goes dark
a bowl of granite or a stone bird
incised by tools the nature of which
is unknown   just that they are metal
and therefore from otherwhere
just that the weight of the bowl
precludes light and lightness
of thought   my feet take a path
I can no longer see   my eyes
won't bring me the bird   only now
has my hand found the stones
I could add to the smooth interior
of my despair   the world goes dark
I look into the eyes of my stone bird
hammers before memory
silence and the world that is not

that is no country
for the unassigned   smell of sunlight
on skin in a darkened room   cabbage tree
shadows dancing in the hologram
on the ceiling   not here
and not there   an in-box the size
of a house   I bury my face
in his neck   breathe in
butter taste of summer corn
sweet plums an apricot almost
perfect in its remembrance
I took the road to anhedonia
forgetting the child on my hip
burying his face in my shoulder
I am that child only that child
looking into the eyes of stone

she flinches
because my hands surprise her
feeling for the soft coat the place to clip
lead to collar   she doesn't see too well
an old dog going deaf but selectively
the nose now only nine thousand times
more acute than mine   the back legs
beginning to fold but still good
for a tiptoe raid on the cat's plate
look at her   black pearl an old lady
out for a walk in the sunshine   slow
and we go into the shadows   stumbling
sometimes on a stone step   the footing
problematic but the maps still delivering
coordinates and forecasts   little dog
black weight on the bed at midnight
love uncloses your eyes   the stone bird
is blind and something I must face
sits behind it making a noise like water

descant on that other madrigal
power tools shaping wood and stone
machining a filigree that falls like moonlight
on the workshop floor   did I dream this
or did I walk out of the house
asking forgiveness and unable to see
anything but my feet entering the shadow
hearing small waves fall over themselves
at the water's edge   now my hand
finds the bird and my fingers trace
the incisions in fantastic replica
not here and not there   an otherwhere
pouring itself through the gap

tell your mama

it's the third of March   your birthday
and you would be seventy nine   my sister
wishes you were around to talk about
making mouths work   oromotor dyspraxia
in the beautiful language of clinicians
I see the little horse projected
in the stairwell by strong morning light
the equinox is on its way
mama we miss you   twenty five years
motor out of our mouths   yes
five foot four and shrinking   we'd like
to have had those years those jokes
those tickings off   the light has shifted
on its bearings   birds eat the figs
apples fall from the trees
let me tell you about the sky-blue stick
whose stories have just begun

Te Kikorangi we could call it
almost as good as the blue from Kāpiti
we eat when the good times roll
pick it up and the weight of the sky
but also its cool panorama
communicate in a nano that sends
your fingers to find the silver collars
the white on blue smile of magnolias
traced out in reverse   and the circlet
hammered with tiny nails by the silversmith
who wanted to leave them proud   fire seeds
talking back to the birds in the trees

and I would know you   looking up
from the page   *by the feel of you*
blue chalk going down on the pavement
as the skies open   *if I were blind*
not a white stick but a sky mama
a pole of wind for the child
waving wildly about in the tree

I open the window after the storm
that washed away the chalkers' poems
almost as they were written   white on blue
the sky smiles again   the stick unscrews
in four pieces   it is a pool cue mama
looking for a good time to come
its stories are at work in our mouths
as the birds fly up in a white spray
that begins their autumn migrations

slow reader

the reports always said
she was conscientious but must learn
to work faster   so she outran
the reading laboratory   got through
tan to aqua and was safe at last
from the speed tests   it was a valuable
lesson   the letters dropped softly
into place making voices sing
or whisper   there was so much to
keep track of   kerning Times Roman
with a sable-haired brush   serifs echoing
celestial geometry   hours of work
for one or two words   about time
she learned space and what lies between
compelling body and soul   light and air
song and dance   big letters flying
from keyboard to screen at a touch
marvellous sarabande   starry gavotte
freehand the camber but understand
weight and measure the way
feet walk in the world and hands
turn pages that take them

out of it again   and the copula
its even-handedness   its tying
of one thing to another so that both
spin along the causeway expanding
possibilities   a non-rival good
an open source a site for sore eyes
quick in its exchange   slow to forget
the illuminations   *psst! psssssss*
sssssssst! pssssssssssssssst!   poem
as event   tied to the smallest detail
cut from the flying vista   Alentejo

Pontchartrain   beyond the river
is where we want to go   Ponte Littorio
shimmering into della Libertà
that kind of hope   that kind of day
that one beside you
offering an arm in the dark

primavera

she was lime blossom   an apparition
walking by the river with her friends
the bridge was under reconstruction
but I got there   corner of Tornabuoni
and the Lungarno   traffic halted   swallows
swept by in bands of seraphic noise
later in a dream she ate my fearful heart

six centuries and the poet's words
fly around us walking to the famous bridge
from our transit camp on Tornabuoni street
where Cartier and Ferragamo sell trinkets
and shoes to make beatific any girl
with euros in her pocket   we're curious
about the Four Seasons on the bridge
made for a Medici wedding some time ago
and standing two at this end   two at that
in a rondo that suggests men play tough
and women are summer and spring
not daring to breathe we look up
at her with the garland and a short skirt
on the poet's corner   yes it's Primavera
we can see the faint line where her head
was reattached in 1961   we know
that's citrus blossom in her hair
ruffled by a wind coming off the river
as the bells begin another sposalizio

she brought back unmarked planets
green and gold ciphers I saw as a child
on the wall of the Eighth Day   that time
beyond our own where she's rounding up
the roses   a dream girl who crossed
the equator on blue stilts and still
tastes like spring medicine to me

behind the wall of an Oltrarno garden
we find magnolias with slender leaves
and jasmine climbing over porticos
above the eschatological roar
of vespas in formation turning into
Via Maggio and making for the ramp
of Signor Ammannati's bridge   1569
which is Signor Gizdulich's bridge   1958
its three mysterious ellipses rebuilt
from original drawings and blocks
fished out of the river or cut again
from the quarry reopened in the gardens
it's a perfect simulacrum
down to the mistakes preserved
by an architect in love with history
and the thumping heart
this morning that's our track
across the river with the scooters
and the kids hanging out on the bridge
with their cameras and phones   hey
someone's texted the girl   ciao bella
just now coming into view along
the riverwalk   she's the one
whose gold sandals flashed past us
in the dark rooms of the Uffizi
five minutes ago   we were joking
about Lippi babes and bottled cherries
she was heading for the stairs
she was out of there with her friends
and something about a poet
green shadows and signs   of things
to come   she was gone
into the crowds of the city we are

I was smoke and rain among the olives
tendrils of the grape were my wild hair
I was sweet water   shadow in the burning place
no wall was high enough to shut me out
now the valleys echo with my crying
he whom I loved is dead   when I find him
we will take shelter in the earth together

around this town of hours we go
visiting the Marias   del Fiore del Carmine
Novella where the soap shop
is floral pastures in a green chiostro
then Spirito Salvatore and Trinita
chasing the architects and the profusion
of their chapels   Florence Nightingale
has a monument in Santa Croce
off in a corner of the primo cloister
chichichichichi   chi chi chi chi   chichichichichi
chi chi chi chi   a quarto arc of water
sprays roses   following the curve
of the poet's voice a cappella
as she draws together
wreckage crocifisso the hammering in
and blowing up the murder stonk
the dissection of thin aortas
and one stray bullet in the campagna
sixty years ago that widowed the bride
on the other side of the world
gentile visitatore   at our school
each hour lasts sixty minutes   such intensity
the pietra serena projects we need
a night off in a campo with other travellers
drinking wine and bubbly water
listening to jazz and an accordion patrol
going up against the treefrogs
rose sellers gather   tomorrow we'll climb
the steps to Piazzale Michelangelo

I was misto and lilystitch in the great
laceration of his heart   he made me
in the image of an angel   look up and see
my face against the ice-bright peaks   then
bring me back to earth with rehearsals
of the life we lived each twenty four hours
when I opened new files on the desktop

from San Miniato al Monte
Pantocrator smiles at the painter sculptor
architect engineer wrapping mattresses
around the belltower he's converted
into an artillery position   out there in the hills
it's happening again   the battalions
pushing forward under clouds of white dust
yesterday they left another cross
on the outskirts of a town   it might have been
Strada   these details are difficult
to establish   only that she had a photo
with sunlight through a wooden gate
and dappled shade nearby   another eight days
and the ghost of the engineer can watch
as forces in retreat blow the bridges
and his beautiful curves go into the river
along with you know who   now we learn
Miniato had his head chopped off
put it back on his shoulders and climbed
up the ridge to expire   is there a date?
25 October 250 AD   the Olivetans
take care of business now   they've been here
with Cluniacs and Benedictines on and off
since 1018   tending the mortal remains
of saints and merchants who wait
for Resurrection Day on the roofs
of their mailboxes and mausoleums
our wandering feet make an ambo
through this city of the dead
its magnolias its star jasmine its electric

weedkiller   Maria Solatrix is ascendant
over the doorway of someone's walk-in
tomb   and under the trees
standing on a kind of wedding cake
two figures modelled from an album
marble shoes and officer's uniform
bringing her flowers   marble gown
in one hand   fingers almost touching
bride and groom gathered in
or about to lead off the dancing   *it's your night*
it's your day   we wept for you
dead 1944 and 45   and think we understand
tears made over into stone   the poem
is two names   it regards the empty sky
as we descend the zigzag and go back
to Il Rifrullo for coffee and a sandwich
spoons clatter   Luciano stands at the bar
singing It's A Man's World   behind us
sitting near one of the open doors
a trio that might be a family is starting
the weekend slowly   fatigued parents
a baby with drop-dead gorgeous curls
squirming on her knee and grabbing
expertly for the paper   swallows dive

keep this book clean

everybody is smoking   the doctor his sister
the little boy the pirate the African king
the duck the dog the pig the monkey and one end
of the pushmi pullyu   we are in awe
of the wicked child who did this   and now reads
the adventure aloud in a small room
above the river as it goes to meet the sea
perhaps if I go down to the seaside I shall be able
to borrow a boat that will take us to Africa
his voice is full of hope   *I knew a seaman once*
who brought his baby to me with measles   maybe
he'll lend us his boat   the baby got well
and the adventure gets under way   in a book so old
its pages are falling out and he turns each one
with exquisite care   has he forgotten
the pleasure of the ink pen attending to curls
of smoke from the ends of cigarettes
and the bowls of pipes   we look between the lines
of each drawing   *lord save us cried the duck*
how does it make up its mind   where the details
are packing their things for a long voyage
all right said the doctor go and get married
but was he right to trust the crocodile's tears
the reader is entranced   as he was when
the secret life of the letters began to take hold
all those years ago   on the rungs and umbrellas
the swings and billowing sails   the arch of swallows
the curve of the sleeper's island   the high gable
of the mud palace   the stomach ache
of the cat's meat man   the weather vane   the king's tongue
the sentry beside the quiet door   the rarest animal of all
on tiptoe foraging the leafy canopy
and this is where smoking stopped
where he became a great reader   attending

to lines of monkeys needing vaccinations
and handshakes   to parrots breaking pigs from jail
and dogs on the trail of fragrant Black Rappee
the last page is gone   who knows where
but it doesn't matter and nobody has time
to look for it anyway   the sea is filling up the bends
of the river outside   the moon looks in
as his voice sets out again   *everything would have*
gone all right if the pig had not caught a cold in his head
while eating the damp sugar-cane on the island

he is the bird who flew away
and settled under a new mountain
among my mother's people   then by a river
with us   we are the kids on the clothesline
the heart of the matter   and we remember
his voice reading the story   *the pantry window*
had been broken by a tennis ball the week before
night after night   the impossible distance
is a swing bridge we cross on winged feet
the queen was away at a dance that night
at her cousin's   or perhaps she was down the hill
looking at the first television set in the district
detail blurs   *but the queen who was just letting herself in*
at the back door with a latch-key saw the parrot
getting out through the broken glass   it is that kind
of world   a line of California quail chicks
follow their mother up the fenceline   a box
of books withdrawn from the public library
comes into the house on the hill   they are tattered
and torn and we turn each page with exquisite care
in an old house in Paris covered with vines   the queen
is trying out her chaud and froid on the controls
of the new French car   *lived twelve little girls*

in two straight lines   imagine   across the river
a bird comes flying   a parrot or a dove
a white goose or quail with their hats bobbing
in the morning sun   it doesn't matter   we will be dispersed
but the words are there on the big songsheet
at the front of the classroom   *me he manu rere*
ahau e   kua rere ki tō moenga   ki te awhi
tō tinana   aue aue   e te tau tahuri mai

peri poietikes

cretan bee persons soar
above the white magnolia flower
how much can you see   they ask
less than I could a year ago   I say
and more than a year ago too   you were
attending to the white flowers with just this
hum   summery   confident   and I
was walking into shadows   afraid to put one foot
where the other would have to follow   bee persons
airy ascenders   your weightlessness
is an inspiration even as I slow to be sure
of the edge   of the dug up crossing   the overhanging
branch   or the children sitting in the middle
of the path   bees   your thunders and lightnings
terrify me even as they assert the way
forward   we were there you say   and now we are
here   a black baldachin folded up in the fizz
of our wings   heartbreak   exaltation
what will it be this bright morning   walking into
shadow   walking into the bleached possibilities
of inhabiting only the moment   cretan bees
you are kinder than the vespas that chased us
over the curve of the Trinita bridge   but your questions
are just as relentless   where are we going
how much can you see   don't you remember
the wind off the river ruffling the little girl's
hair   cretan bee persons   you seem
to have done it again   the deep breath
that is my first stick   the blue cue that is
my second   the third that reads the world
at my feet   and this   the fourth corner of wind
holding up the sky   unsayable   limitless
a pool on the edge of a cliff where people
come and go   some of them sit on the parapet
some look for lemons on the trees
lining the water in tubs   and some dip

their toes companionably   watching the ripples
and the beginning of writing across
cool air on a hot day   we were there and now
we are here   I see more than I did
and the bees in their beautiful skirts
dip and lift above the white flowers saying
yes there is more and that is our job   now go
and bury the possum washed up on the beach
before someone steps on it unawares

how did that get in I ask   the wind
brings a terrible stink   the poem is suddenly
smelly and unclean   and nobody
will come back for the poisoned bones
anytime soon   the bees are silent   the cicadas
take over in their massed chorus that begins
in the grey light before dawn   around poetics
you must walk without fear they chant   all measure
is with us in the trees and the undersides of leaves
dropping cool messages on bare skin
cicadas I say   you roar and you shirr   how is that
what I am learning   apo koinu
they reply enigmatically   jump from the join
that is a possum in the corner
and one hundred per cent humidity   cicadas I say
you are not very clear   is there another way
of hearing what you have to say   silence
then off they go again louder than ever
about measure you swim in the blue water
making and remaking the shapes of air
about poetry we fly in a cloud of noise
sometimes it is a white flower   sometimes
a carcase hung under the wharf   when the bones
are clean they will be brought into the house
around the heart   we fly   and sing
surely this is something you can understand

more like wellington every day

hey poems   we are free to go
a book is one thing   the night sky
another   pack up your things
and throw them into the back seat
the long drive is a pleasure we duplicate
with our heads full of riotous quiet
thinking between and speaking sometimes
as the beloved country rolls by
how many journeys does it take   how many
of us with our google maps   and someone
waiting at the station   or guiding us in
to another local grid   the child on the train
is writing a four-letter word in green chewing gum
stuck to the seat in front of him   thoughtfully
he removes it   chews   tries it on the window instead
he's the ghost of the kid in the Health Camp
at Ōtaki   hating it like all the others and compelled
to write letters that begin Dear Mother
I am having a very nice time

tsunami warnings in place this morning
after a 7.9 south of Tonga   the car radio searches
for a clear frequency   falls away as we climb
into the rhyolite heart of the island that is
a lake or the place where the hook tore
at the flesh of the great fish   take your pick
flatto peaches   elephant heart plums
table grapes the way they used to taste
and peppers shaped like the horns of a bull
the rental flies along   collecting wisps
of cirrus   grass seed and crickets
tweeting   white scut of a bunny
on the track beside the highway where we stop
for a pee and look out at ourselves
sailing over the Mōhaka Gorge   past Waipunga Falls

roadworks and endless tag with horse floats
converging on the bay   how many journeys
to make visible the railway house
with the pram outside and the baby yelling
happily   his big mouth wide open
and the young parents with flashing smiles
on the front steps at Willowpark Rd
close to the house where Marama and Rose
feed us early tea and memories that catch
sometimes in our throats   even the dogs
seem to have met us halfway   making sure
the story is nose first they saunter
through the wedding in the olive grove
and spring into laps that promise food or love
or both at once   she wanted to give him back
the glass he gave her all those years ago
he told her it should stay with her   bubble of light
weight of the moving sea   sound wave
dear mum I have a weather shell at camp
the prisoner writes and we know
what he means   what he is holding against
his ear   then carefully dated
7 March 1934   we had a very bad earthquake
on Monday night   I was first to wake up
I thought I was in a rocking chair
did it shake you too   in her arms again
a small weight and so far away
the years between are full of spin
that hurt them both   famously
before another wedding   christ mother
you look like a Parisian streetwalker
white-hot spaces the family remembers
forever   we swing out of the Tukituki Valley
and drive to the carpark below the peak
the sun hops over the skyline

where distant waves are travelling no faster
than they should from the horizon
and the morning is free of harm
poems   we are momentary guests here
where my father was born and learned
as he went   how to make vapour trails
in watercolour   *the mountain the river*
on a sky the colour of bones

heartland

spirits bay

the joker in the orange vest
is baiting up an electric kontiki
his mate is in charge of the line
has been up here three years or more
working on the roads   Saturday off
and they want to try this side   the kontiki
is good though sometimes the breakers
hammer it   twenty five minutes
in the battery   enough to get a fair way out
fish for tea plan a or plan b   their mate
is surfcasting from rocks below the point
their ute has an orange light on top
the kontiki a little red flag   up on the ridge
a black horse watches us
then walks off into the mānuka

she went back to Te Paki   turned south
for the run down the beach   a comedy
with driftwood and tarpaulin under the wheels
tide coming in and they got the car out
marching chocolate and toheroa leaving behind
the swish of vague stars above ti tree
scratched out lines on Exquisite Bond   trying
to see the flying-off place   the pathway
of spirits a rope and basket affair
pretty near worn through twenty years
back   trying to see past melancholy
love is your overwhelming theme   yes
but why leave it to the horse and the stars
or the line of white plumes shaking
out there where the currents meet

the gateway has been shifted
the buildings erased   only the lighthouse
remains near the end of the spirit pathway
where the prophet heard the snuffling   peropero
of the dead as they passed and saw
a great house above the cliffs   crash barriers
write on the cambered bends
of the new road   sealed now from the top
working back to the junction and perhaps
ten kilometres to go   the three capes
wrangle as they have always done
and down the cliff comes that old kahika
still holding fast to the rock and refusing
ever to flower   a destiny and a song

listening

pīhoihoi the spiralling song   a pipit
and who will give the skylark a name
to fling against the cliffs   I cannot see
but my ears are open   have been opened
to the song and its destinations
spiralling backwards into the abyss
from which we will emerge   shining shocking
ready to start on the long walk south
alpha and omega I am with you
but I have changed hands   ostriches
an olive farm big windbreaks small chalets
unwinding the bird in my throat

in the city of words the wild man
wakes and knows he must leave
the warm bed the arms that detain him
where he has always wanted to be
this is not romance but death   the city of words
plunged into darkness   swans clattering
into the sky above the lake   which gleams
and turns back to the beloved head
at rest in the room before dawn   the wild man
ungovernable and meek as milk
all in the opening of one eye   has left
us now   he is near the on ramp and won't stop
even for the lament his brother makes
from wood glue a guitar and a kick drum
even for the voice that has held him
so long where he wanted to be
and now reaches into the sky   wordless
black wings crying   love pain hunger
I have changed hands alpha and omega
unwinding the bird in my throat

kōtare out the car window   here
wraith blossom and scrub cattle   there
dustclouds on the way to the fish farm
gone bust by the shallow harbour
one kotare two kōtare three kōtare four
songlines for idiot ears   everywhere
velocity in the November sun
dog snuffling its way around a bend
gamboge yellow   not sure how much
to take literally   and what can be left
for the others   orange cones
fill my eyes on the road south   alpha
and omega changing hands   unwinding
the bird in my throat

degli angeli

I saw my angels   they were beautiful
beyond compare   flags snapping above the headland
combed blond by wind   they were sitting
each with disaster in a small pocket and they were
so beautiful in their resistance to the idea
of letting it fall into the world   they were meeting
in a room with light powered by small engines
perfect examples of resonance   and the distribution
of energy to this evolving flute   that tapering cup
in the hand of something like god   or the sound
of wind across hillsides   how to say it   they were
complete they were not defined they were still
and they were moving each moment   closer
to each other and further away   I saw them   they were
beautiful   they were the winds of heaven
in a small cup   unbreakable and looking at me

never dreaming

they came in a wave cloud   in bonnets
in gowns ballooned by the westerly flow
the slow circling of isobars   clockwise
counterclockwise   each with majuscule
definition   turning to the others
as sail pilots look for the marked channel
marvellous sarabande   starry gavotte
points on a map drawn by geometers
forgotten or disappearing into the beat
of a warm pulse   they call out
Dinah Elizabeth Hannah Jane   each of them
huge against the sky and turning around
to hook another's arm   Hannah Elizabeth
Dinah Jane   my daughters I left behind
will you forgive me   my sons I will bury
on the steep hillside   lend me grace
and a strong heart around the new house
sisters angels   clockwise and counterclockwise
we turn on our passage over the sea   behind us
the biggest iceberg yet to escape circumpolar
currents   ahead the three capes wrangling
beside us voices crying   Rina Hēni
Irihāpeti Hana   and our hands folded
carefully around the green shoots   sweet briar
crimson china   our undocumented fingers
weird with grief and the future   rose wreaths
floating with the tide on a harbour of jade
voices on the deck   playing draughts   playing
the governor   making a cartridge case
Rina Hana Heni Irihapeti   bring your feet
across the sky   looking back looking
ahead   makers of wreaths and small shrouds
ladies of the wind   come ashore
we have you almost at anchor again

almost between the heads and beating
into the westerly flow   fiducial angels
never dreaming where your names
will take you as the seas begin to rise

lomu

and now the other black dog
grinning and wagging   bat ears hoisted
nose to the wind   eater of gravy-soaked
tea towels   pie thief rabbit digger   co-pilot
riding shotgun in all the vehicles   deaf mute
weight on all the beds   now the black dog
sleeps under the avocado at Weld Road
wrapped in an old blanket and keeping an eye
on the three pigs' ears luck has brought
his way   now the black dog sleeps

olive

the day of the explosion they postpone
her arrival   two men walk out and agony
begins its clinch   we crouch by the radio
unable to help   thinking *they could all be dead*
hoping for a miracle twenty nine times
the size of a mountain in the eye of a needle
stitching blue heaven to green earth
let them walk out let them walk out alive

it is too dangerous   when they bring
her at last three days have gone by   each
more terrible than the one before   angels
look out of the eyes of this dog who is here
because I am blind and the world is huge
with possibility   we walk her in a raw wind
not knowing we shouldn't   a mistake
that costs but is not the end of the world
under the dark mountain of sorrow

when they show the dust blasting
out of the portal for fifty seconds   we know
there is no hope but listen as machines prepare
to enter the shaft   today I learned how to comb
how to check ears eyes nose teeth and all over
for the baseline that is hands on a warm body

when the drill breaks through   the images
show that nobody reached the oxygen refuge
when they find a cap lamp still flickering
in the camera's eye four and a half days
and a kilometre in   we go out for the first time
just around the block   only to hear
there's been another explosion

dog   I hold my breath as you take us
into the world I can't see   each day
a little further a little more command a little
sliver of hope under the dark mountain
where fear waits with its next fuse
and rescue is unlikely any time soon

from all over the world gear and advice
pours in   a third explosion sets the coal burning
deep underground   *the trapped miners*
become *the lost men   the men who lost their lives*
and finally *the entombed men*   now they gag the mine
starving the fire of oxygen and the violent language
of despair cries out upon us   threading the path
between light and darkness pain and rage
care and the undoing of everything we cared for

my dog how can you move with such grace
through these days   pulling sea and sky along
with you under the red-flowering trees   mixing it
up and down the road with all comers   this is not peace
but motion   ten thousand people looking up
the valley to a dip in the ranges while someone sings
You'll Never Walk Alone   not peace but motion
what is her name they ask me and I say
she has been here since the start   her name is Olive

experiments (our life together)

here is my experiment with the dark

we run to the top of the street and crossing it
become aware of the fountain's lip and mosaics
under water pink blue hyaline we step through
the foot bath yes the gold leaf is holding on

here is my experiment with stars

it is a dormitory on the top floor this two o'clock
the babies wrapped loosely in sheets asleep
and somehow not falling out of their little moulded beds
the blinds drawn down the afternoon heat

here is my experiment with humours

aqueous the home movie
tears on the lens and always the return
to rivers their flumes and fumaroles
so plural so carrying so carried away

here is my experiment with light

which leaves me now the dear shapes
gone to sound the end wrapped around
the beginning a piano in a dark room that is
quite what it is like and never the same

here is my experiment with river

memory and the wind ruffles her hair
there are no fences on the sun only a truck
bouncing on the flood its wheels gone and us inside
scared to death and still steering

here is my experiment with rain

we swim and let the current take us
where it will which is some toehold around
the corner under cliffs of black honeycomb
the saltwater pool afloat on its concrete rim

here is my experiment with amygdala

in the morning we find a bar and marmellata
as the sun comes up and the streets are cool
a slice of duomo at the end of each stony block
an orchestration a theatre of the mind

here is my experiment with immanence

who was waiting there who was asking me
to look at heaven from the end of a dark wharf
and when I did when I raised my empty eyes
the city was there a necklace of light a horizon

here is my experiment with periphery

who was asking me not to forget
rippling scales in another room a gallery
at the top of the stairs a cupola a vault
a canopy a river of light on the ceiling

a brief history of time

the book slips past my ears
on the flight over   three hours
following the sun folding up corporeal
reality and I'm not finished as we begin
the descent into   earlier   tray tables
secured seats in the upright position   not
a molecule lighter or less perturbed
than the cold air under our wings   we step
back in the same day and forget an hour
the spooling voice entered and can't leave
or leaves many times without us   going on
split or spilt from departures arrivals terminals
the book slips by and I am not done

she came out of the crowd a stranger
leaving the city we were entering   please take
this she said   it's good for seven days   but
the metcard she gives me expired yesterday
a platform is a crossing place   alight depart
the gift of a stranger is not always legible

in one glissade we see the waiter in his brocade
waistcoat through the glass at Grossi   his brother
tall and dark walking into Self Preservation   their cousin
on her way to work at European around the corner
where we sit outside in the sun and wind with balloon
hearts waving foolishly over our heads   listening
to the lived detail the trail that will take us from Cumulus
to Gingerboy Sichuan House to Saint Ali's Journal to
Auction Rooms My Sister Says Il Fornaio Brunetti Bar Fred
and phone-ins from places under consideration or just off
the map they draw for us and change a moment later

the young people into whose lives we have tumbled
whose city we enter with passports that declare distance
even as we close our arms around them   the young people
we were in another life without trepidation and full of bounce
darlings beware be happy and beware   look after each other
your voices once more in our ears your heads bent over
another app another cloud another touch pad   there's a tram
in two minutes ten minutes twelve minutes to take us home
across the dark river on a freezing night in July

a little earthquake on the platform at Princes Bridge
to match the shiver underfoot in Auckland the night
we were packing   shadows at Alimentari   the zip my fingers
could not learn   the forest of misery on the walls
around us   rain and sun a monkey's wedding   a book
or a tram slipping by with that sweet shifted clang sampled
from ancestral bells and played through a speaker
the young man in the park with his head in his hands
the young woman adrift   running down Collins Street
with Charles Buckmaster   the voice of Lydia Valerio
leaving Torino di Sangro oh mother I don't know where
I'm going   for a flat above a tyre shop in Collingwood   or who
I'll meet when I get there   the Eureka stockade thrown
ninety floors into the sky running red lines under our feet
rumbling bass surplus to requirements real or imagined
and people in a glass box moving out from the side of the tower
darkened walls made suddenly translucent   the sound
of shattering glass   who cleans these windows anyway

we fill a big table here a small table somewhere else
jumping from story to story   who could remember it all
the soundshell the lovers by the fountain the pigeonnier
the observatory the winding stair the view due north
to that other shrine of remembrance and its magnolia path
above the Sangro   we sit with our children who are meeting
each other for the first time   a confusion of pronouns
perfectly clear at the table which gathers but does not snap
the collation   the collection   the warm collocation
now drifting to its next appointments   à bientôt à bientôt

à bientôt till Friday till Thursday till tonight
the swan-necked decanter the quiet dog creeping
onto a friendly knee by the fire   the mezzaluna
rocking out along the bay or through the fine crust
pulled from the hot oven   the mezzaluna of doubt
of two hands of cutting it fine   as the doors close
the bell clangs and the drunk begins his hyena call
to the black universe then charms a small boy in a paper hat
it's my birthday too very same as yours same as you   I am
going to see my friends all my friends tonight   seven days
of crossings going off like steel drums   again and again
we say goodbye and walk into Hill of Content where the book
opens itself to the very page I was on   real or imagined
starting over on the way back against the turn of the earth

matapōuri

the magpies come to the corner of the house
and talk all morning to the figure on the flag that hangs
on the orange wall   my fingers trace the sewn words
COME WIRELESS   a voice fills in the rest and flashes
from my good right eye   ALALU   give back the black and white
but it's the orange I want   morning sunlight on the wall
the birds and their qwardle   the bells in the painting
of KARANGAHAPE ROAD in a shed on the side of the hill

nothing more joyous than a dog in water   except two dogs
paddling along beside us in the waist-deep water   so clear
the estuary at full tide   feet sinking through sandy crusts
WHOA   the dogs turn back and we drift with the current   WHOA
to where waves are coming over the bar   WH-OA   soft landing
against the side of a sand bank   as in the dream one moment
out of my depth one moment a toe on the bottom   I open my eyes
underwater   so clear   everything as it should be   kicking along

post MERIDIAN the wall of sound is cicadas   the shade sail
flaps one manta wing on the hot concrete and I'm off   barefoot
to find the London planes whose whitewashed trunks
will lead me   step by step   out to the point   an ALLÉE
a path to walk ALONE   counting and listening   marking off
each tree there and back   the dog running free with her nose in
RABBITS   sharp gravel springy kikuyu   ALONE and seeing
the same pathway in moonlight under the morepork's loony call

vanishing points

The Fascicles

In darkness, redcoats marching out to the Pekapeka block. It cannot be true. But imagine
for a moment it is. Two women stand almost in the same place which is the rim of an old
volcano. One is remembering her father stepping out of the blockhouse when she was a
little girl going down an Irish road wherever they were just then. The other is stunned by a
memory of fruit falling in a dark garden, soft sounds in long lines or sweet juice over stops
and starts. An orchard? A volcano?

Neither can be sure because the ground is shifting. They pick themselves up and go on,
unaware of the jolt that has put them on the same page and will now tie them to this
place, whatever it is. One watches the shadow of a long skirt ripple ahead of her in the
afternoon wind. The other has almost reached home with her quire of clean white paper,
walking uphill from the shops around the quay. There is dinner to get, the washing to be
folded, but no children so there is time for everything connected or unconnected with the
red jackets of the soldiers moving along the Devon road in darkness or in daylight.

I love him, she thinks. I vocate, says the other, haptic with risk. Each sits with her head in
a pool of lamplight, mind and fingers flying over the mending of works and days, now and
then, yes and no. They have torn up the pegs, they dispute the sale, they build a fighting
pā on the ridge to the south west, Te Kohia, and draw fire from the valley running down
to the bony sea. This is the beginning, a transfer of words for deeds with tails as long as
kite strings in a clear blue sky. She folds the creamy sheets of paper and pulls red silk
after the needle that pierces and pierces the fold, binding, stitching, tying together the
new pages of a little book, a booklet really, pliable, plausible, something to fold down and
begin writing. The valley in the dark, the ridge abandoned. The lamplight, the flashing
needle, the words I will write from the orchard that is a volcano. For you have shown me
the valley in the north and its river running down to the sea where redcoats, militia and
volunteer rifles are landing to begin the work of destruction. One moment I am in a dark
orchard. The next I feel the ground shake under my feet. I am a soldier's daughter, fled
away from my father over the sea and finding him again here in the new land.

What shall I write? Where should I bury my flashing needle with its red silk tail as long as kite strings in a clear sky?

I found it
in a dictionary
and look
it comes true

these days
with peaches
with intricacies
of step
      and step

afternoon tea
with dancing

2

Prune plums bloom blue in the leaves. A holiday morning, the cutter making her way over the harbour towards Quail Island with a load of picnickers, bonnets and shawls and a row of bunting just visible under the billowing sail, high voices of children palpable to an attentive ear. The distal edge, a fingernail of sea and sky in this new place, late summer and the leaves of the orchard still thick with fruit.

My name is Dorcas Carrell and I was born in County Clare on the edge of the great western ocean. When I was nine we sailed with the regiment to Canada, when I was eleven I lost my mother and my sister there. Quebec, Sault Saint-Louis, Montreal, back down the seaway to Halifax and out to St John's, another edge. We were always moving, out and back, out and back, the sound of waves breaking on a rocky shore. I was eighteen when I married one of the gardener Carrells, twenty four when we reached his brother's acreage on Jackson's Road above the harbour in Lyttelton. We fell easily among nieces and nephews to whom I taught their letters and how to draw the delicate shapes of plants

they brought for my herbarium. Seeing their pleasure in the folios on my worktable,
I thought to make small books from butcher's paper tied up with string in which they
might draw and paint for themselves. We are gardeners, bedding down below the ferny
ridges, looking south across the harbour to an island in the arms of an island, west to the
rim of the caldera and beyond to the distant mountains. We are orchardists, bringing
ashore the sea-wracked saplings, binding them to volcanic soil, making shelter against
winds sweeping off the ice. I am a gardener of stars, I tell the children on clear nights.
See, here is my garden and there are the stars, stellata, stellaria, stellissima. My pretty taxa.

It is afternoon. I see the children collecting sea eggs on the island, picking their way
among the rock pools, squealing as the octopus shoots away from a hand that has come
too close. The gaff does its work and they hold up the purple shadow still dripping
ink and writhing, its three hearts salvo, salvo, salvo. Bodies lying in the fern above the
Waireka Stream, the beachwalkers under fire, regulars at the Whalers' Gate turned and
gone back to town, bluejackets after dark storming an empty pā. Who tied the notice to
the gate of Henry Brown's farm, clear cursive lines flapping in the wind? Whakarongo
mai, whakarongo mai, e te iwi. A sign, a pānui, a protection. Listen, listen all people. The
road to the Minister and friends must not be trampled upon. White scarves. Aunt Dorrie
on her hillside above the sea. The bows of the cutter lift as she turns into the wind.

> plum under the blue
> bloom
>   prunus
>   spaces
> the sky came through
> saying
>   the dark leaves
>   open
>   summer's
>   catalogue
> we began
> keeping
>   and can't
>   finish

3

Dear winter it is 5.15 a.m. I take the short line, snapped or cut but never broken. Out of the cradle endlessly rocking I follow the long line, a valley running down to the sea. But rocking has stopped and the ships, Erebus and Terror, are caught in ice. The dark rule of history skips a beat and it is winter on the harbour looking over the rim of the caldera at distant mountains. It is winter in the northern valley where the fortresses Onukukaitara and Puketakauere stare down the flooded river, asking for trouble.

Rocking has stopped and the ships, Erebus and Terror, are caught in ice. Slowly they circle the frozen islands, and their names are mountains as well as ships. Slowly they circle frozen islands that are not freed in spring by the cracking of ice that rushes downriver to the seaway. Slowly they circle in a sea of ice that holds them fast, Erebus and Terror lost to us whether mountains or ships or figures of dream circling just beyond waking. I heard the ice come down the river in spring, says one. I saw the snow mountains beyond the buckled rim of the harbour says the other. A body of water, says one. A sea of ice, says the other. Erebus and Terror at the bottom of the world. Erebus and Terror at the bottom of the sea. If I wake from my dream of winter, will I see the river in flood, will I see snow mountains pouring over the buckled rim of the harbour? Will I see my lost mother and sister?

Dear winter it is almost light and the guns have opened fire in the flooded valley, anxious to redress looting and killing on both sides. A garrison moves out and is split in three between the two hills, Onukukaitara and Puketakauere. But the defenders lie in rifle pits outside palisades that shudder under the impact of each new explosion. Onukukaitara the bait. Puketakauere the hook. The defenders lie in wait. When the trap springs it is too late to get out of the gully, it is too late to get out of the swamp, it is too late to retreat with the dead and the wounded. The black cross of Te Ātiawa flies in triumph on the hilltop this morning. The river is in flood.

I am Dorrie in Lyttelton, daughter of a soldier, wife of a gardener. My mother is an armful of lilies, my sister a stone angel. Erebus mother, sister Terror, you pour over the rim of the flooded valley this morning.

darling the boat was a murder
though I must smile and say it was nothing
out of the ordinary   the world turned
upside down and beloved faces veiled
behind ocean spray   you won't remember
the voyage from Halifax but mama's white face
haunts me still and the rocking of a boat
is the rocking of a dark cradle in my brain

Emily and Her Sisters

a beginning

Someone in the distance, a voice on the wind. Mesembryanthemum australe and Adiantum (Sugar Loaves, Taranaki). Light pencil. Samolus repens. 1860. Iceplant, maidenhair, primrose. A little spray and the big breakers washing ashore at Back Beach or leaping at the base of Paritutū. I had written a long letter, she said, but on reading it over thought best not to send it.

catherine

She is a watercolour. Mauve silk in bright sun and out of the wind caught at the corner of a composing eye. She moves papaver against the light and words fly from every selvedge of her floating veils. It must have been such fun to get ready for a wedding in such a hurry. Dear little Katie took it and was dangerously ill. I collected a great many burnt articles and made cloth shoes for the children. Their thin arms and tear-shaped ribs. Their bare legs. Their anther feet. They ran wild among the rocks and streams stoning crabs and paddling tin canoes. He made bows of supplejack and arrows fledged with iridescent feathers picked up he said in Mama's duck pen. Hoydens he called us. Pirate Jennies. Tribe of hubbub ripped skirts and raspberry mouths. Fuchsia and sophora tucked up together in the wedding album and only three of us mindful of the place they came from. Its littoral hideouts, its forbidden gullies full of boulders and birdsong. The arrow found its mark, the bird fell. Draw us together, she said. I am like the active verb to be and to do, I am too necessary an appendage to be left out.

a fine girl

She is always there, the fine girl born on the boat and taken from them five days later. There, did you not hear, they are conveying our darling to the deep. Back she swims and never leaves off calling to us, mirthful, tantalising, one who knows the next step and the one after that. One who was on the beach at Waitara and when he wouldn't listen flung herself between his head and the bullet. A fine girl following the shell back to town through rippling winter sunlight, crying like a gull in the jade green waves. She is another watercolour. She is a covered cup. Bindweed, mānuka, native bluebell. Mama temporises. I long to take a walk with the dear children. The forest is behind me and the sea in front, but I dare not venture in the former for fear of losing myself and the beach is often too exposed to high winds making us almost blind with the iron sand and the great waves dashing against the rocks. Then she has more courage. I have seen a beautiful waterspout and the whales sometimes but not often. She is always counted, the fine girl lost on the outward voyage.

frances

She is my rebel soul, my other self, the one who draws me out and folds me away. She is a brush tipped with paint, a Conté crayon poised above white paper. She is running after Frank Standish, wearing out her heart on him, waterscape, landscape, natural rock archway destroyed by the quarry opened up for breakwater construction and at last there was safe harbour for landing in. Frances, fourth daughter, my sister across the sea when I despaired of ever coming home. Who kept Papa and his harp happy on the cart taking them both to the port. Frances who sails back to the rough shore, then the sheltered one. Who stays in a sister's house and dies there, sleeping not beside Frank but our ghostly brother. Voices on the wind crying his name, the two of them elbowing each other as in the old bed where we slept top and tail giggling uncontrollably until Mama put her head around the door. A native orchid in flower against a dark background. Slender leaves with panicles of delicate white and yellow flowers. Earina autumnalis, springtime autumn fragrance in the forest. What could you be but watercolour to me? We will not look back, it is too painful, she said. And I cannot look forward, it is too dreary. We will watch the gauzy clouds float by. A snowy veil athwart a sky. Of deepest blue. I left.

mary

Points first a pair of scissors drops from the wall she is scrubbing and cuts open her arm. Blood gouts, children scream. Emily just off the boat. Emily in the doorway with her carpetbag, her easel and her painting box. Aunty, aunty, aunty. We bind the wound, we calm the sobbing children. We get the cases of paintings off the cart and to the back porch. Has it ever been different we ask ourselves. Fire and sword, chaos and ruin. I watched her sail back to the fatal shore with her trousseau indivisa. Mary so full of hope in her clematis veils. Mary climbing plumose, Mary collecting and growing, her hands in muck and ground truth. My lightness in springing over every little obstacle, she said. I swung down in a moment. We picked up the torn and trampled papers, we put the boxes in storage and sent the harp by schooner to Papa. Mary in Eltham, Mary at Awatuna. Mary in Havelock with her orcharding boys. Mary journeying to farewell Kate, Mary in Waimea, Mary in oils. Mary the traveller, outlasting us all and returning to take up with Kate on the hill at Te Hēnui. Between them they see that the boxes and paintings are safe and will come to light. The married names, she said. A rhizomatic insurance and a joy. Puawhananga. Some authorities leave out the h.

augusta

She is a dark archive. My hands go in and out of the boxes looking for her and finding only rain in the night. During this time a moth dies in a pool. Ethos and pathos. Elevated slightly and the artist has drawn the drop-shadow on the ground beneath. Shadow and light. Without them the most perfectly executed drawing will fail. Astelia grandis. Listen to a piece of music. Agaves and allies. Listen to it from another room. Order Asparagales. A spilled jar of ball bearings. Rolling cloud. Toetoe. I saw her on the riverbank at Mōhakatino, drawing perching lilies and saying don't you see they will never find me. I have destroyed the map, I have given the wrong name, I am over the edge of the world, ungazetted and fading from view. She said as long as she had any I should have some flowers for the grave. My hand goes in and out of the bushes without injury, she said. For of course I did not undeceive him. There is low composition with shadowy plants growing toward a lighter upper half of the page. There is the gorge and the coast. Soft hyphen. Look, holes.

ellen

She is the girl on the path running to meet three figures on horseback outside the gate
on the Frankley road. Her mother stands in the doorway of the house, its garden and
fences neat, the mountain on view through cleared bush. The sun shines, the sheep and
bullocks are fat. Ellen my seventh daughter. The veranda posts were made of fern trees
and the creepers grew rapidly round them which gave a pretty appearance to the cottage.
Dear Corbyn at the gate with Kate and Emily. Before the house burned, before I took my
daughters all but one to Nelson, before my son was killed. The family chain so roughly
severed, she said. I wish Augusta and Ellen would make me some crochet edging. I wish
you would send back the box with my poems and letters for copying. One purple flower
spike and three pink ones against sea and coast, below them Stilbocarpa leaves and
flowers. Youngest and most intricate of compositions. Flowers now called Aralia lyalli,
Ligusticum latifolium and Ligusticum antipodium. It was you for whom the gift of the
sewing machine meant most. Five-fingered jack and two anisotomes. Who could see us
making books as well as gowns and children's costumes with that flying wheel and its
piercing needle. Run for the gate, little sister. Run as far as you can down the road and
don't look back at the mountain getting ready to strangle your happiness.

leaving

The deck heaves. Her three important baskets have been brought on board among the
boxes and trunks of the family she is working for. The baskets hold everything she will
need from this point forward. A memory theatre. An art museum. A life of the mind.
Also the rock arch and spray drifting. She gathers them up and goes below, trying not
to look back at Paritutū and the islands black against a stormy sunset. The sea swept
them off the rock. One body was washed ashore but the others were never found. Listen.
When I went down to the cabin again the vessel was fairly on her way. Our darling.
I went to bed to prevent myself from being sick, she said. The Screwpalm family. The
vessel an immense churn and I a lump of butter continually thumped about in it while
the waves splashed like gallons of buttermilk. A wind muff, a dead cat. Velar filaments
most probably modified arms. Dreadful noise and motion of the screw. Relict, the only
surviving member of its order. Someone in the distance holding out a small gloved hand.

from Figures in the Distance

1

It is so dark I am certain the sun has gone. Canyons, archaic, abyssal, open in front of me and the flutter of leaves is lost in the roar of traffic overhead. I take my way, start out walking, thread the path that passes a trickle of water underground and then a spiral ascending. Present tense, imperative mood, no light. Doves resume their conversation in the trees outside the window. The scent of star jasmine creeps over the sill and is gone in a moment that is not quite memory, not quite now. Scent of a frangipani tree backloads into my nose at this spot each morning, not quite now, not quite then or even there. Start out walking, count and measure, find the letter and lift a finger from the glassy surface. These are the steps, this is the footwork, thread and clue near walls of stone and overhanging trees. All present, all sure. And the sudden reticules of light. Imperative. Urgent. Sol going down in flames.

2

But it is different each time. Eyes of a woman, your oceanic eyes, marine eyes leaning into afternoons of wind. The white shell path crunches underfoot. Location. The wind is face on, then slant. Location. There is no image but the lightfield is immense, at once cerulean and granular. Waves dash, spray wets the path ahead and behind us. Wind plays in the trees. How much pōhutukawa bloom is falling? Will I feel its touch against my face if it is? The finger lifts, the letter appears. One more touch. Location. Acoustic shadows slap hands, drink milk, roll into the wind and become lost in its rough and tumble. The words appear from nowhere. Who are you beside me?

3

Every day you play. Metrosideros excelsa. With the light of the universe. Plumeria, a temple ghost. Wind falls away and railings gleam in the shadow showing me where I am, later and darker along the waterfront. I lose my footing one evening on the simplest of steps and go down in a heap, crying out loud. Bruised in strange places, not all of them available to reason, going down, getting up, stepping along. Rosemary brushes my face, an overhanging feijoa takes off my hat, the odd scent of pōhutukawa drifts at the edges of the shell path. Every day it is different. In soft damp air someone is searing beef or making a sauce. Garlic in hot oil shimmies into the frangipani coming over the road at this spot each morning. A temple ghost, I said some days ago but found another name by asking, casually. Do you remember that tree, the one that flowers in spring and is not a real frangipani?

5

A white rose. See. A white rose stencil. There. A white rose stencilled there. Signalling. A white rose stencilled on asphalt. Marking. A white rose stencilled on the footpath. Dividing. A white rose stencilled on the footpath to show juncture. Or continuation. A white rose showing juncture. Here is one. Go on. Here is one. Go on. Here is one. Now turn and pass the coffee drinkers, their laughter and their dogs. Their open doorways. Their cry of gulls and clatter. Their arches. Their caves. Go on. Another rose, to show. Another, to go on. To show where (a rose), to show what (a rose), to show how (a rose). A white rose bringing juncture, bringing continuation. Long shadows walk beside us, four legs and two. Two legs and four. Gulls cry. Last white rose. End of the line. I will throw my eyes up to heaven and bring back the blue bowl of the sky.

6

So it is still possible to step ashore on the islands of vision and say I remember. It was like this. To find the planetary contrejour of lightshades and low sun against the western window. To make a glissade of light from the ripples spreading across flat water. To catch light and to make it sing. Here is a cat sitting on a rock by the sea, a marine cat who crosses the road each morning. Here is a man on a bike who calls out my name as he passes. Here is a runner who calls her small dog to order. Max, come along. Here are two people frying tomatoes on the beach. Here is a song chalked along the pavement beside the flowering trees. LOOK IN THE NOOK OF THE CROOK OF THE BRANCH OLIVE AND GREEN, POHUTUKAWA PLAYS THE BLUES. A pack of ocean swimmers disappears around North Head. The pool is underwater. Now hear how the cruise ships play, coming and going from the harbour, the channel, the five notes that warn small craft to get out of the way. Eggs and bacon and tomatoes in the pan. A man with a fan on his back hangs from the cords of a parachute, drifting out to sea. His sanguinary lady takes the old cat home.

7

From the waterline, masterpieces of the oral and intangible heritage of humanity float on their poles against the sky. Day by day, hoist and fly, the flag of France (Charlie Hebdo), the flag of Colombia (Carnaval de Negros y Blancos), the flag of Cuba (island revolution). Who knows what they will fly tomorrow, or the next day or the one after that. Kite surfers full of hot air sweep to and fro on the harbour. The same breeze drops tōtara into our noses and karaka berries under our feet. Rise up singing. Rise up dancing. Rise up and make carnival. There is the flag of interlocking spirals on black and white. Hoist and fly. There is the flag of a spiral as long and lazy as a green wave rolling or fern above the sea. Day by day. There is the flag of the new year, smoky tōtara and sweet karaka lifting the small bird, a tern with a silver fish in its beak flying home at sunset. Oral and intangible. Day by day. Hoist and fly. The arrival of the cavalcade, the voices on the wind or against the sky. Flags for the new year, a game of football on the beach that might go on forever, hoots and cackles and the exhibition of ferocity, stamping and pawing and falling flat on its face in the waves to thunderous applause. Rise up singing. Rise up dancing. Rise up and play every day for the oral and intangible masterpieces of humanity.

12

Shaking hands. She gives me her paw, and when I stroke its smooth surface I feel her toes flex and the nails close over the hand that is holding hers. I do this again and again, to feel her hand close on mine. This is as good as listening to her one-two-three one-two-three lapping at the water bowl, threes and fives, fives and threes, before I remember Gertrude Stein's little dog and what listening to the rhythm of his water drinking taught her about the difference between sentences and paragraphs. That paragraphs are emotional and that sentences are not. The dog wins a soluble fish for her demonstration of emotion in front of the Modern Poetry class. She is more interested in the microphone than the water but we loop her lapping and amplify it for close listening anyway. Yes, paragraphs. No doubt about it.

15

She stops dead so I know there's something in the way. Perhaps it is a truck parked across
the footpath and connected with what sounds like someone chopping wood. I call out
but nobody answers. She won't go on and she won't go around, so we cross the road. But
I want to find out what has spooked her here at the corner of the domain. We retrace our
steps with a helpful young man who can see no obstacle and nobody chopping, just the
swift brush of olive trees in need of a street-side trim. She takes us through the problem
stretch, clearly no longer a problem. I thank the young man, who was on his way to meet
friends kayaking around North Head, and tell him we'll be fine from here. And so we
should be, but at the next crossing she takes us on what turns out to be a diagonal, and
suddenly I realise the street and the fall of afternoon light is all wrong. We get out of
this by going back to the corner and reconnecting with familiar patterns. Later I realise
that a car parked too close to the corner has confused her, turning 'straight across' into
something longer and less useful. Later still I realise that the sound of chopping wood is
the bowling machine at the edge of the domain firing out cricket balls that someone is
hitting into the nets. She's been trained to look for hazards. Good girl.

18

In he comes, bouncing and sweaty, to borrow a towel and go swimming at Duders. Voice
out front, key in the lock, just passing through. A voice on the phone from an airport
far away, saying early morning is the time to go and see the ruins outside the city when
there's no one else around. One heading for the beach each morning with a thermos
of coffee and that same ragged towel. Breakfast. The other drinking something from a
coconut on a beach in Mexico. One in this city, one in that city, two brothers crossing
the sea. Camper vans gather down at the bay. Two people sit with their feet in the waves,
looking out to sea and drinking wine from glasses they fill from the bottle hung off the
side of their aluminium deckchairs. The house at the corner has been flying a tricolore
since the Paris attacks. The house next to it is flying a flag that says Happy New Year.
Here's a man walking up the street dripping wet and asking if he can stick his nose into
the buzzing magnolia flowers at the gate.

24

Blind swimming. Let your hands find each doorway, let your fingers trail the edges of furniture, the tops of balustrades and the walls of hallways with their punctuating spaces. Where there is space you may pass, taking care not to move too swiftly or beyond the compass of your hands swinging from that moment to this. You will be fine but don't daydream and lose the sense of where you are. Everything is very close. This is useful but now you must find ways to extend your reach. One of these could be swimming. After all there are fewer obstacles and no steps to fall down in the water. There is however the problem of too much space and no punctuation. You set a course and push off, swimming in a more or less straight line. Except that it's not straight and a second swimmer is needed, someone to tail you and call out course corrections. Eleven o'clock, he says. One o'clock, he says. One o'clock, meaning the left arm isn't holding its own. Eleven o'clock, meaning put more into the right arm. And keep kicking. Keep counting. There is nothing better in the world than a body slipping through water. Eleven o'clock, eleven o'clock, he says. We are nearly at the buoy. Why is it never twelve o'clock except in the silence of a straight line? Keep kicking. Keep counting. Every surface is a space to pass through.

25

I saw my hand against a sunlit wall. Just for a moment.

28

They are out on the point having a quiet beer in the dark, the young men who grew up here and like to revisit old haunts. The moon is up, the evening is calm and free. Boats row out of the harbour with wings of fire. A door opens and a crowd of old people pours across the road down the steps and into the sea whooping and hollering. How old? I ask. Very old, he says, the young man who is telling the story. They were ocean swimmers on a midnight training run following the path of the moon towards North Head. He swears they were every one of them naked. Not that you could see much. But it makes a change from the parrot man and his two companions in their large hats. Or the woman in her sackcloth rummaging the bins at night with old Charlie. Or Walkie Talkie striding the pavements ceaselessly, once in a hoodie they were too scared to reclaim. Or the woman in tulle pushing her pram about the streets when they were little, her daughters dressed as fairies. The stencilled monarch butterflies that appeared in bus shelters and on walls one night when nobody was looking. The pink and purple house. The salt devils. The wooden toys and the palm-tree mugs sitting on the kitchen hatch. This evening a pack of Sea Scouts is rafting up in the waves, shrill voices of children scrambling from one kayak to the next then it all falls apart as someone goes into the water. Shrieks of delight from the other side. This morning one of the float planes is taxiing across the harbour beside us, then the pilot opens the throttle and it takes off into the light breeze from the south.

29

I saw the Māori Jesus walking on Wellington Harbour but his pool in the shadow of the museum was drained for repairs and the words were no longer lapped in fishscale light. I saw John Baxter in the pool ecstatic in arcs of water he was splashing over his father's words on the day the writers' walk opened. I heard the mihi that was sending Wellington Harbour over the father's words. I heard the camera catch water light and send it to the eyes of beholders who were a great crowd on the waterfront that day. We took the train as far as Woburn, crossed the platform and came back along the side of the harbour. We took the ferry to Day's Bay and back riding on the top deck and talking about other excursions. We had a dance at the mardi gras and kept walking along the waterfront to Roseneath. When we turned back there was the young woman walking towards us with bags full of produce from the market. Look, holes, she said.

30

We know what the dog of tears will do next, he who has been trailing the woman standing on the balcony looking up at the sky. She is the woman who wept, he is the dog who licked away her tears. They have gone on like this for some time, the only woman who can see and the dog who is now more human than he wants to be. His nails scratch the wooden floor. His belly is as empty as everyone else's but he does not mind. He is walking towards the woman on the balcony. When he reaches her she will bring her eyes down to look at the ruined city and become blind. Everyone else will have their eyes back. She will have the dog of tears. The dog will bark holes in the last page of the book and lead her through one of them. There they are, the dog of tears and the woman who wept. His nails click on the rough stones. She who can no longer see begins to tell a story. They pass the street of crocodiles, the pool of tears, the hill of forty days and the hill of forty nights. They pass the little seahorse in its salty pool. They pass a white rose, a black swan, a blue biddy. The dog kills another hen and they roast it over a small fire. They can hear the sea, its fronding on smooth sand, its talking against rocks, its clapotis bouncing off stone walls. What might we not do with the hot bones dripping fat, she says. Two birds rise into the air on wings the colour of ash. Did you hear that she asks the dog licking away the salt on her cheeks.

coda

the wedding party

I

I see them walking
their horses down the Carrington Road
white satin bows tied to each bridle
white satin shoes laced with ribbon
sidesaddle in the summer morning
buttonholes of wild rose and forget-me-not
from the clearings at Hurworth
the wedding party advances into history

2

I found words
rough winds do shake
the darkling buds on their candelabra
dusk and spring on the Carrington Road
the magnolia, the mountain
my eyes were sealed up
but my ears caught the sound
of japonica and persica, the plantings
the mountain, the magnolia
jasmine all over the ponga house
clematis horse on the garden fence
we rode and climbed and looked out
skimming up trees to perches
settled in advance
by age, by who could walk the bar
and swing into the lower branches
the elm, the red gum, the rimu
but not the pōhutukawa
whose pathways baffled our monkey hearts

3

on a winter's night
a traveller
coming by the Carrington Road
to the ruined houses at Hurworth
could read in chalk on a broken shutter
e nga tangata katoa o te taua
all the men of the troops
kaua e tahuna tenei whare
don't set fire to this house
hei moenga mo nga tangata e haere ana ki Waitara
as it is a sleeping place for the people going to Waitara
na Te Tapihana
the match flares
throwing light for a moment
on the words of a chief of Ngatihikairo from Kawhia
travelling overland
between loss and strategy
leaning tawa fallen across the road
lookouts under the trees
hangi pit under the front windows
bookcases thrown down
but the house stands and is not burned
a question in need of a reply

4

at sixteen I dreamed
in colour and could finally translate
small pieces of Carrington Street
my mother in a sunlit kitchen
newspaper clippings pinned to the curtain
six cherry trees frothing in the driveway

Latin homework waiting downstairs
quomodo barbaricos auxiliares discerneremus
how we might distinguish friendly natives
mihi videtur indusium vel tunicam subalbam signum idoneum esse
it seems to me a white under-tunic could be an appropriate sign
not Caesar but one of the horsemen
from the wedding party
not three months later
writing to Auckland by the overland mail
hoc Latine (canum more equidem) scripsi
I have written this Latin (dog-style though it is)
ne nuntio intercepto literae in manibus hostis accederent
lest the messenger be intercepted and the letters fall into enemy hands

5

mihi videtur it seems to me
the words come flying out of the dark
ngā mihi warm regards
between two waves of the sea
two languages, two trees
throwing shade over the Carrington Road
this fine morning
the war party sets out for Waitara
the wedding party, finished with church
rides for Mangamahoe and breakfast
at the Meeting of the Waters

Notes

"on white you fall," "Watermelon World," "27"
Part of the chapbook *Sound Pitch Considered Forms*, with Don Austin and Clemens
Rettich (Vancouver, British Columbia: pie and or press, 1984).

"Merylyn or Tile Slide or Melete"
A response to Merylyn Tweedie's *Nicola or Floral Tile or Betty* (1989), floor tiles,
photocopies on fiberglass cloth on vinyl wallpaper, coated with epoxy resin, 459 x 428 cm.
Lines from Janet Charman's "the print kiss" in *red letter* (Auckland University Press, 1992)
enrich the conversation.

"Where exactly are we?"
A ribbon text commissioned for the exhibition *Now See Hear! Art, Language and Transla-*
tion, Wellington City Art Gallery, 1990. The title references Dinah Hawken's poem "Bal-
ance," from *It has no sound and is blue* (Wellington, N.Z.: Victoria University Press, 1987).

"Micromelismata"
Part of a text commissioned for *Amending the Vulgar*, edited by Mary-Louise Browne and
Ruth Watson (Wellington, N.Z.: Vulgate Project, 1992). A wall text was part of the 1991
exhibition *Word for Word* at Artspace, in Auckland.

"Blue Irises"
Material quoted includes text from the following works. Fleur Adcock, "Ngauranga
Gorge Hill," in *High Tide in the Garden* (Wellington, N.Z.: Oxford University Press,
1971). Mary Barnard, *Sappho: A New Translation* (Berkeley: University of California Press,
1958). Ursula Bethell, *From a Garden in the Antipodes* (London: Sidgwick & Jackson, 1929).
Eileen Duggan, *New Zealand Bird Songs* (Wellington, N.Z.: Harry H. Tombs, 1929),
Poems (London: Allen & Unwin, 1937), *New Zealand Poems* (London: Allen & Unwin,
1940), and *More Poems* (London: Allen & Unwin, 1951). Bernadette Hall, "Constructing
a Landscape," in *Heartwood* (Christchurch, N.Z.: Caxton Press, 1989). Dinah Hawken,
"Balance," in *It has no sound and is blue* (Wellington, N.Z.: Victoria University Press, 1987).
Robin Hyde, *The Desolate Star* (Christchurch, N.Z.: Whitcombe & Tombs, 1929), *The
Conquerors* (London: Macmillan, 1935), *Persephone in Winter* (London: Hurst and Blackett,
1937), and *Houses by the Sea* (Christchurch, N.Z: Caxton Press, 1952). Anne Ridler, *The
Nine Bright Shiners* (London: Faber & Faber, 1943).

"cairo vessel"

A free variation on K. A. Kitchen's reconstruction of a fragmentary text in *Poetry of Ancient Egypt* (Jonsered, Sweden: Paul Åströms, 1999).

Journey to Portugal

Italicized lines between poems are for the most part taken from my reading of Fernando Pessoa made before and during the journey and written on verso leaves of the notebook that tracks an excursion to Portugal in the early summer of 2004.

"work for the living"

A response to the death of Hone Tuwhare (1922–2008), celebrated Māori writer and Te Mata Poet Laureate, 1999–2001. Tuwhare's elegy for his close friend the poet Ron Mason was read by poet Murray Edmond at Tuwhare's tangi in Northland in January 2008. The Yorkshireman is poet and novelist Russell Haley (1934–2016); the bearer of pūriri leaves is actress and writer Frances Edmond.

   Mirabile Dictu collects poems written 2008–2009 during my laureateship.

"primavera"

The poem remembers Dante's Beatrice by way of Alan Brunton's "Getting Back the Bitter for the Sweet" (1974) and Mary Stanley's elegy "To B—" (1944), New Zealand poems with connections to Florence.

"keep this book clean"

A tattered copy of *Doctor Dolittle*; my father's voice reading aloud in the dreamscape of childhood; words ("Me he manu rere") sung by massed five-year-olds.

"spirits bay," "listening," "degli angeli," and "never dreaming"

Originally part of the chapbook *Northland* (Auckland: Pania Press, 2010).

"The Fascicles"

Chris Pugsley's "Walking the Taranaki Wars" (New Zealand Defence Quarterly, 1995–96), James Cowan's *The New Zealand Wars* (Wellington, N.Z.: Government Printer, 1922–23), the Ngā Māhanga pānui of March 1860, and the files of the *Taranaki Herald* and other newspapers (1860–61) supply historical background and certain voices here. Others, including Ron Silliman, Walt Whitman, Emily Dickinson, and Fanny Howe, cut in from the PennSound podcast *PoemTalk* (2007–14).

The poems closing each section are mine, repurposed for their role in the imagining of a nineteenth-century woman writing on the outskirts of empire as bitter racial conflict erupts around her. We are connected (she is the sister of my great-great-grandfather). We are disconnected (there is no trace of her beyond a few bare dates). But she came to the place where my poetry begins. She heard about war in places I knew as a child. What might be chanced? What double binding of circumstance might produce one to (or for) the other? If ever you need to say something (the voice is Dickinson's), tell it slant.

"Emily and Her Sisters"

Later she became a well-known botanical artist and wrote lively diaries that showed how difficult it was to make a living teaching and painting in the 1880s and '90s. But Emily Cumming Harris (1837–1925) was a writer all her life, and it is the young woman of 1860, already a confident, archiving poet, whose trajectory I trace here. Like her contemporary Emily Dickinson, Emily Harris copied her poems into letters and sent them to friends and family members. Unlike Dickinson, whose almost 1,800 poems were discovered bound in small handmade manuscript books after her death, Emily Harris's poems have largely disappeared. But not quite. At Puke Ariki Museum in New Plymouth, New Zealand, are two handmade booklets (fascicles), and in them are two poems about what it was like to live under military occupation in the town in 1860. Two poems and their contexts make visible a vanished world.

Other key images are six works by Emily Harris in the collection at Puke Ariki (one for each of her sisters), inwreathed with the responses of four contemporary women writers and what can be made of other voices in the archive. Thanks to Anna Boswell, Makyla Curtis, Bronwyn Lloyd, and Erena Shingade for their generous contributions to the project.

"Figures in the Distance"

Here is the compass rose with its thirty two points of wind and some constellating figures going around in circles. Someone walks toward a blackout that seems perpetually delayed by voices on every side refusing to let up or let go. Perhaps this is a future. Borrowings and influences occur throughout. Thanks Rita Angus, Hugo Ball, Christian Bök, Jorge Luis Borges, Pam Brown, Alan Brunton, T. S. Eliot, James and Robin Fryer, Ida Gaskin,

Mary Gauthier, Ernest Hemingway, Lila Hobson and Meadows Rendel, James Joyce, Tessa Laird, David Lees, Federico García Lorca, Ern Malley, Pablo Neruda, Ezra Pound, Marcel Proust, José Saramago, Gertrude Stein, William Carlos Williams, Virginia Woolf, Dorothy Wordsworth, and anyone else I might have missed inadvertently.

"the wedding party"
Māori and Latin texts are quoted from *The Richmond–Atkinson Papers*, Volume 1, edited by Guy H. Scholefield (Wellington, N.Z.: R. E. Owen, Government Printer, 1960), published one hundred years after the Taranaki war that is their common ground.

Acknowledgments

I wish to acknowledge the support of Auckland University Press, the Caxton Press (Christchurch) and the Holloway Press (Auckland). Thanks also to publishers Jack Ross and Bronwyn Lloyd (Pania Press) and Clemens Rettich (pie and or press) for their chapbook productions. The poems included in this selection were first published in journals, books, and websites in New Zealand, Australia, Canada, the United States, and the United Kingdom, 1984–2019.

About the Author

Michele Leggott was the inaugural New Zealand Poet Laureate (2007–2009) and received the Prime Minister's Award for Literary Achievement in Poetry in 2013. Her collections include *Vanishing Points* (2017), *Heartland* (2014), and *Mirabile Dictu* (2009), from Auckland University Press. She coordinates the New Zealand Electronic Poetry Centre (nzepc) with colleagues at the University of Auckland, and has co-edited Alan Brunton's selected poems, *Beyond the Ohlala Mountains* (Titus Books, 2013), with Martin Edmond. In 2017 she was elected a Fellow of the Royal Society of New Zealand.